Legacy:

The <u>POWER,</u> Purpose, and Passion of Divine Appointments

Chuck Schumacher

Dedication Page

I DEDICATE "LEGACY" TO MY CHILDREN GRACIE, MICAH, AND NOAH SO THAT THEY MIGHT HAVE A CHRONICLE OF MY LIFE'S JOURNEY AND NOT HAVE TO RELY ON FRAGMENTS OF INFORMATION TO RELATE FUTURE TALES FROM MY MANY EXPERIENCES. YOU HAVE PUT UP WITH COUNTLESS EPISODES AND STORIES OF DIVINE APPOINTMENTS OFTEN HEARING THEM MANY TIMES OVER, BUT SEEING THEM IN PRINT WILL HOPEFULLY BRING BACK FOND MEMORIES AND HELP YOU TO KNOW MORE ABOUT YOUR CRAZY DAD AND HIS PASSIONATE LOVE FOR YOU AND THE JESUS HE PASSIONATELY DESIRED TO SERVE.

Table of Contents

Preface

"Paga"/ Hebrew for intercession: "A chance encounter or an accidental intersecting where God supernaturally places people on our hearts."

Jesus always told stories to make a point, and often times, those stories were personal encounters that began as coincidences and ended up becoming "divinely inspired" meetings that would change the course of history. Wherever Jesus went, it seemed that He always got involved in people's lives through the strangest of circumstances. For example, John the Baptist was minding his own business, doing what he loved to do—namely baptizing. Along comes Jesus and John finds himself doing the greatest baptism of all time. Peter and Andrew were minding their own business fishing, when they were recruited into an army that would radically change the world spiritually, socially, and politically. Through other chance meetings a leper would be cured, a blind man named Bartimaeus would be healed and toss his beggar cloak (a license which allowed him to beg), because he no longer needed it for begging. Incredibly, a woman caught in adultery would be forgiven, and a well would become the scene of reconciliation between a Samaritan woman and Jesus, a Jew. Also, a hated tax collector would come down from his perch while observing Jesus pass by, and have dinner with Him.

And if that wasn't enough, a thief hanging on a cross, was promised eternal life one Good Friday evening.

Jesus made Evangelism seem like it should be an everyday experience. By example, He taught His disciples that if they would be available for God to use, their testimonies would transform hearts and change nations making them true History Makers! Their legacy would be the changed lives, which would be the fruit of their love and example.

The Psalmist in chapter 78 revealed the importance of legacy.

> "Oh my people hear my teaching; listen to the words of my mouth. I will open my mouth in parables, I will utter things, things from of old- what we have heard and known, what our fathers have told us. We will not hide them from our children; we will tell the next generation the praiseworthy deeds of the Lord, his power, and the wonders He has done."
> Psalms 78:1-4

Asaph, the writer, was challenging the reader to understand the importance of those past events in the history of Israel and how together they became a road map or legacy for future generations. He saw the importance of leaving a clear understanding about the great things which the Lord their God had done for His people. That is what legacy is all about.

Joshua had the same idea in mind in chapter 4, when he commanded 12 men to bring 12 stones from the Jordan River and place them on dry land as a monument and reminder that future generations might come to know the legacy of their forefathers and the great God they served.

I believe that the greatest part of anyone's legacy is the story line that develops from point A to point B. I've often been asked by people who knew me years ago how I ended up doing what I do? It is here that my legacy unfolds. It is here that I can reflect upon the joy of knowing Jesus Christ, and my subsequent journey in serving Him.

We are all a tapestry of life's experiences, and when we allow those experiences to shape our destinies, what we are becomes a reflection of who we were and most importantly, what we shall become.

This book is my legacy. In writing it, my prayer is that my family and co-laborers in Christ, as well as future generations, would be blessed by the God that I have humbly tried to serve in the midst of many failures; a God who has blessed and nurtured my soul by the divine appointments that He has allowed me to experience.

Introduction

"Do not neglect to show hospitality to strangers, for by this,
some have entertained angels unaware."
Hebrews 13:2

You may have a hard time believing that many of these events actually happened. I would too, except that I have humbly experienced and lived through every one of them. Until I personally met Jesus Christ, and He began to reveal Himself to me in ways that only experience can validate, I would have most certainly been a scoffer like most. But the facts don't lie and experience speaks for itself.

Recently, I took the time to look back over the years and examine my journey. As I did, amazement and joy flooded my thoughts as I realized not only the exciting life that I have led, but the people that God has positioned me to meet. I found myself asking, "Why me Lord?" In my youth I could never have imagined that someday I would leave my state, let alone the country, and travel to some of the places that I have been blessed to visit.

What was so unbelievable you might ask? First of all, I would never have dreamed of flying 24 hours while traveling to India, and then have the privilege of speaking at a conference to thousands of Hindu converts. There, I witnessed a woman who had been blind since birth, receive her sight, while another woman, only minutes from death, arose from her sick bed. I would have never envisioned a visit to Damascus, Syria and the opportunity to walk on the "Street called Straight" where Saul had met Jesus. How could I ever forget standing at the Damascus city wall where Paul was lowered while escaping from his enemies? It was there in Damascus that we worked alongside our sister church ministering to Iraqi refugees streaming across the border into Syria. Incredibly, it was there that I had the opportunity to play a role in leading one of Saddam Hussein's government officials to Christ.

I would have never dreamed that someday I would climb the Eiffel Tower in Paris, or even stand in front of Buckingham Palace in London; nor could I have imagined being in downtown Jerusalem for Israel's 50th anniversary celebration as a nation. And let me tell you, that was quite a party!

I have had the once in a lifetime experience of seeing a rainbow over Mt. Ararat, mounting a camel at the pyramids in Cairo, Egypt, and then navigating through a narrow crawl space to view a pharaoh's hidden tomb. There, I learned the true meaning of claustrophobia!

How could I ever forget being asked (with only two training sessions) to assist in surgery on a medical mission's trip to Ukraine, when I had never handled a scalpel in my life?

I have seen the ugly face and hardships of war up close in the land that God gave to His people, Israel. There, from the foothills of snowy Mt. Hermon to the glittering blue sea of the Galilee and from the limestone walls of Jerusalem, to the beaches of Tel Aviv, as well as from Bethlehem to Jericho and from Masada and the Dead Sea to Eliat, I have traveled the land of Abraham, Isaac, and Jacob many times training and mentoring young leaders. I have prayed at the Wailing Wall in Jerusalem and stood in Melula, Syria (the last village on earth where Aramaic, the dialect that Jesus spoke, is still spoken).

Through an invitation by a friend and former holocaust survivor, I had the sobering experience of participating in the 50th anniversary of the liberation of Buchenwald concentration camp by American soldiers in Eastern Germany in

1945. There, with 5,000 ex-prisoners and 38 American veterans, I realized the horrors that made this death camp one of Germany's worst. It was at Buchenwald that 70,000 Jews, Christians, and other political prisoners were gassed and cremated in Hitler's ovens. It was also there at the anniversary in a small German café, just outside of the camp grounds, that we led an American soldier to Christ. He was a hero who had been one of the first American Rangers to enter the death camp gates at Buchenwald. Sadly, even after 50 years, he was still haunted from the horrors and human suffering that he had seen with his own eyes. He had never shared his pain with anyone, not even his parents or wife. But thanks to a divine appointment, he was delivered and set free from his memories! Several months later, he spoke in our church sharing his story, but this time as a free man!

I had the privilege of being part of History Maker 1, in Cyprus, which brought together Arab and Jewish Christian youth from nine different nations, including Israel. There we saw the Holy Spirit break down the walls of hatred and fear and replace them with Jesus' reconciling love.

My life was forever changed by working at Ground Zero in New York City after the attack on September 11th and the incredible experiences with survivors and workers that God placed in my path.

All of these experiences have had one common thread: each of them led to meeting somebody unexpectedly and in the most unique of ways, impacting their life and mine. As I look back, I see a tapestry of God's love and incredible plan. And with amazement, I still find it hard to comprehend, knowing my shortcomings that He couldn't have found someone better to do the job than me. Yet, I see all of this as a blessing from God, and all because of His love for me and my choice to make myself available. Sometimes we fail to remember that God is not a respecter of persons; He is simply waiting for our willingness to respond to His call. But before all of these doors could open, I had to first come to grips with the Bible being relevant in my life. After heart felt searching, I soon began to identify with many Bible characters. There was Thomas the realist, who responded to Jesus' words of comfort in John 14 by asking a logical question, "Lord, we have no idea where you are going, so how can we know the way you talk about?" Philip, the pragmatist, expressed my personal point of view in the same chapter. "Just let us see the Father and that will be more than enough; just give us a sign Jesus!" Judas, who was seeking truth, asked Him, "Why are you showing yourself to us and not the whole world?" Soon I began to get excited when I realized that those simple followers of Jesus had the same critical mind as me.

I've always been a pragmatist (dealing with the facts) and realist; (a) plus (b) had to equal (c), or I wouldn't buy into the premise or argument. If I couldn't see or touch something, it had no validity or merit as far as I was concerned. To say that I was a total skeptic was probably too harsh, but the word "supernatural" and those who believed in supernatural experiences just didn't fit into my way of thinking.

During my transition between high school and college, and after a long search for purpose and meaning in my life, I prayed a prayer that several friends had challenged me with, a prayer that would change my life and destiny forever. I prayed, "God, if you do exist, and I believe that you do, let me see your supernatural grace one time, and then I will surely believe." I was not challenging God as much as crying from the depths of my heart. I had tried it my way long enough and realized that it just wasn't working.

I don't remember whether I coined the phrase "divine appointments," or heard it somewhere. All I know is after I surrendered my heart to Christ, He took this broken and empty vessel and filled it with love and a passion to reveal Himself to others. I have always struggled with a sense of unworthiness, and usually have shied away from meeting new people and other uncomfortable situations. But then it began to happen; maybe I was waiting for that supernatural experience where dead people rise and the seas part. Instead, I began to meet people "accidentally" and see those "accidents" blossom into incredibly divine appointments, which began to profoundly change my philosophical way of looking at life and thinking. I could never have invented what I was about to experience. And like many of you now wondering, I never could have believed for myself that I could make a difference in anyone's life through a "chance" encounter and travel the world while doing it.

Now, more than 40 years, countless stories, and one simple prayer later, His marvelous forgiveness and love have defined my life and led me to share "The Power Purpose and Passion of Divine Appointments" with you. This is not a "how-to" book on making divine appointments happen. If that were possible, those appointments would not be divine. My heart's desire is to encourage you that, if you are willing to be used, He will lead you to people in such a way that Evangelism will be a natural part of your daily walk, and the lives that have been touched by your caring and love become your legacy or deposit left behind.

Keep in mind "legacy" is defined as "the sum worth of one's life passed down to the next generation." Legacy is the treasure of what we have lived, accomplished, and deposited, as an inheritance, into the lives of those following in our footsteps. "Legacy" is our story, our journey, our fulfillment, and our history. It is our gift of experience provided to others with the hope of inspiring their own great callings and adventures.

I will never forget the power of that one simple prayer, prayed forty years ago, which has filled my personal legacy with fulfillment, joy, and meaning. As you read these pages, ask the Holy Spirit to take control of your destiny that you too can leave a legacy filled with divinely inspired moments that make a difference in the lives of others.

Chapter 1

Ruined for the Ordinary

"If you are willing to be used by God, He is more than willing to open incredible doors."

I 've often been asked about my experiences travelling to foreign lands as a part-time missionary representing the Gospel of Jesus Christ. And after some of the stories and divine appointments that I have shared about through the years, one might think that my experiences have been one Godly encounter after another. I wish that were true, but what I can say through experience is that when you do step out in faith and challenge your fears, you are ruined for the ordinary! Life can never be the same again when you have experienced God's extraordinary power and love. I could never have become the person that I am today, if I had not had the experience of meeting so many people in foreign lands and had them become as close as "family." Like the Apostle Paul, I can say that, among men, I am truly blessed.

Therefore, as I begin this amazing journey with you, I want to share directly from my journal, the adventures, blessings, and challenges that shaped my very first trip to Ukraine in 1993. This is raw footage, so to speak, and reveals those first days and experiences of a journey that began when I said,

"Yes," to God's calling on my life and church. As I have revisited that first experience, what stands out is God's faithfulness to what He showed us and the completion of what He promised. I also learned that what He often reveals will take place in His timing and not mine. So let's get started on a journey that began April 15th, just after Easter celebration at home, a journey that ruined the ordinary in my life forever.

Thursday April 15th…Today was rather uneventful. We left Cleveland at 8:10 am and landed in New York, where we had a layover of 8 hours. I talked to a couple who were also headed for our first destination-Schiphol airport in Amsterdam. They had a son in a cult and were rather distraught. We had a good conversation, and I offered them what advice I could. The flight was uneventful and smooth, and soon we would land in Amsterdam and have a two hour layover. I see people from every country and background imaginable. It is beginning to sink in just what I have gotten myself into.

It is Thursday 2:00 pm Ukrainian time, and we have gained 6 hours. We have just arrived at the airport in Kiev. It is like walking from the 20th century back into the Wild West! We got off the plane in the middle of the runway and were loaded onto what seemed like a cattle truck; our luggage was put on a hay wagon. There are soldiers with assault rifles standing all around. They look so young. One particular soldier is passing out visa information that we have to fill out. He is giving everybody a hard time…I don't think that he likes Americans. I just acted like a dumb tourist, which isn't too difficult, and so he pushed me on just to get rid of me. Customs was another challenge. We had to wait in a long line, which I am learning is a Communist thing, even though the country has been free for a few years. Old habits die hard. Everything is becoming a hassle. Our luggage is lying exposed on the sidewalk for anybody to pick up, but God seems to be doing a good job of protecting it…☺

3:30 pm…Now the next challenge is about to begin. We have one hour to get to the train station and are going in two separate taxis, which have to be "pre-World War One" vintage. The other taxi has gotten stopped at one of the many check points, which are everywhere. I am with our interpreter named Natalie, and we are patiently waiting at the train station with everyone's luggage. The other taxi has pulled up with 10 minutes to spare and the train is about to leave. So, we had to literally run with our heavy suitcases for a good 10-15 minutes to make it to the train. My heart was beating so hard, and the soot from the train engine's chimney was making me gasp for air, but we made it to our coach just before the train began to move. It is Easter week in Ukraine, and the trains are jammed. Because we were so late, the conductor has sold our tickets, but Natalie talked to him, and he let us on after she paid him a bribe. Welcome to Ukraine! Actually, she had argued with him for 15 minutes and had to outbid someone else for the tickets. Quite likely, she had to out bribe them too. If we hadn't gotten on, we would have had a five hour wait in the train station which was filled with homeless people and bums. It is not that I mind being with bums, but after standing in line all day, being pushed around by soldiers, running a marathon to catch the train, nearly suffocating on coal smoke, and finally jet lag, I was ready to collapse and just wanted to get to our destination.

4:30 pm…We are so thankful to get on the train but have found that our coach seating is a small enclosed room about the size of a tree house with no air and very dirty. We have struggled for a good half hour to get our luggage, including eight suitcases, above our bunks but were just informed that we are in the wrong coach. We had Ukrainians angrily yelling at us in their native language, and all we could do was nod our heads and smile.

8:00 am…We have arrived in L'viv Ukraine and it is Good Friday morning…a journey of approximately 15&1/2 hours. I have come to fondly describe my train experience as my "Ukrainian night in hell." I will explain.

As a child, I always enjoyed when my grandma would take me on a train ride to visit relatives. And so I was excited to ride a train through the beautiful Ukrainian countryside and soak up the culture. The only problem was that it was too dark to see anything, and the culture consisted of a cramped coach, which reeked of sausages and beer. My friends and I were separated because of the ticket problems, and I ended up with a young couple, who spoke no English and several drunken Russian soldiers in the next coach who sang all night long. Most of those sitting a short distance from me had not yet been introduced to the modern age marvel of deodorant, and so I, my clothes, and everything I touched developed a very unique blending of smells. I spent at least the first ten hours wide awake missing my wife and kids and asking myself just why I had ever agreed to do this.

4:00 am…It is the middle of the night, and I have to use the restroom facilities but don't know where to go…I had been warned to not expect the Hilton, but what I just found was the most unique experience of my short history of riding Ukrainian trains. First of all, the "bathroom" could not be used until the train was 4-5 kilometers outside of the city, because everything dumped directly onto the tracks. But it didn't seem to matter, because the walls and floor were covered with **** from top to bottom. Oh the glories of Socialism and government run trains. I soon began to get a whole new love for democracy and free enterprise!

8:00 am… We have finally arrived in L'viv and are arguing with the people who unloaded our luggage over what we owe them. Of course, we never asked for their help, they just grabbed the suitcases and then wanted money. Across from me, one of our team members is arguing with a taxi driver over how much he wants to charge us. Because we are Americans, everyone we meet only sees one color—green, and what's more they all think that we are rich. We have met a young man named Taras, who will be one of our interpreters; he really impresses me.

9:30 am. We just arrived at the apartment where we are staying, and I met a young man who wants to go pass out Bible tracts; this should be interesting…Well, we just got back from witnessing on the streets of L'viv... One of our many encounters on our adventure was a drunk who could barely stand up. What was amazing was that he took most of our tracts and began to pass them out also. Whereas, some people would not take them from me or the young man, the old man who reeked with the smell of alcohol, gathered a crowd of people that readily took the tracts. My only thought was that if the Holy Spirit could use that man, He could use anybody!

This afternoon was a real adventure. We went to an art fair in the center of L'viv, where master oil painters come in from surrounding areas to sell their portraits. I know that this will become a favorite shopping place for me. There are so many neat gifts and all sorts of painted art of landscape and buildings. We ended up passing out Bible tracts, and here, the people were so hungry for truth. One older gentleman, through hand gestures, asked for two tracts for his son who is in the army. Who knows what seeds God is planting here? I am having a chance to use my Russian language skills, (or lack thereof). At least, I am able to communicate a little. Some of our team needed a restroom, and so we looked for the nearest one, but there was none. Finally, we walked into the local post office. There, I asked the lady selling stamps, if they had a bathroom. She pointed me towards an unpainted door. When we walked over and opened the door, the stench was incredibly overwhelming. Behind the door was a dirt floor area the size of a small room totally covered with piles of "you guessed it." I went back to the stamp seller and told her that that was the most disgusting thing that I had ever seen. She looked at me and laughed, telling me that I could take it or leave it! Finally, we found a restroom in a restaurant that consisted of a hole in the floor and two places to put your feet while you squatted. The ladies, who are part of our contingent, are learning to love Ukraine more by the moment. I miss my family so much, but I am beginning to catch the vision of my purpose for being here. Taras has been with us all day and is a true servant. He has a wife, Lilia, and children but is intent *on meeting our every need at the cost of being away from his family.*

Going home from the art festival was interesting. Half of our group went with Taras, while the rest of us rode in a taxi. Well, it was like a taxi. You see in the Ukraine, you can flag anyone down, and for a few coupons, the driver will take you anywhere. We were blessed to get some guy who was mad at the world and backed it up with his driving. Where there wasn't a road, he made one! He was traveling around 70 miles per hour on roads with potholes that were sometimes several feet deep. He wove between oncoming traffic like he didn't want to see tomorrow. And when the traffic came to a stop, he just went on the sidewalks and cut through fields until we came to Taras's parent's apartment. We were greeted at the door with warm hugs and asked if we had a fun afternoon. I could only reply that Ukraine was everything I expected and then some and could not have taken much more "fun!" Today, my prayer life and thankfulness for every breath breathed rose to a whole new level!

Saturday April 17th...I will never forget today. We were picked up at 11:00 am and driven to a small village 2 hours away. There again, we were welcomed by a wonderful Christian family with such warmth and love, that we felt just like we were at home. It brought back so many wonderful memories of my grandparents, Tessy and Stephen Demchak, who grew up on the Poland Ukraine border. As we walked in the door, there were so many smells from my childhood; pierogies, pigs in the blanket, and mashed potatoes and pork. And because it was the day before Easter, the table included a beautifully decorated basket with Easter bread or "pasha" and colored eggs...

After dinner, we went to another home to pray with a small boy who had polio. The mother was overcome with emotion and cried the whole time kissing us over and over again. Next, we stopped at the home of a teenage girl who had run away from home. She was overwhelmed with deep hurt because her fiancé had left her and married someone else. What could we do but share the love of Jesus and pray that He would take away the pain. Again her mother burst into tears, and as we left, handed us a loaf of Easter bread. It was so surreal today seeing everyone carrying their baskets of bread and brightly colored eggs to mass for the priest to bless for the Easter dinner. While it was not part of my culture, it tied me one step closer to my heritage, family legacy, and roots; something that would happen over and over again on this trip.

My Russian is really improving, but sometimes I know just enough to get myself in trouble. This morning I tried to ask one of the teenage girls at the apartment where we were staying if she had ever visited America. But because I messed up a few nouns and verbs, it came out something like "Do you want to come to America and live with me?" When I realized what I had said, we both laughed and laughed, but her mother didn't think that it was so funny!

Tomorrow is Easter Sunday, and we are taking the train to another Ukrainian village where I will be speaking for the first time. God help my broken Russian to make sense!

Sunday April 18th…What a tremendous Easter! We had a wonderful service, and my Russian actually began to come back to me. It hadn't been since high school and college that I had studied the language. We had a great time passing out tracts and bubble gum to the kids at the church, but I did mess up in one area. After church, we were praying for people, and I didn't realize that men weren't supposed to hug women for obvious reasons known only to them. Well, I had spent the whole afternoon hugging these little old "babuskas" or old grandmas, until someone finally informed me that I wasn't supposed to be doing that. Oh well, so much for love and building relationships! But what would happen next would truly just about break my heart. We went to a youth prison which was filled with over 100 young men 13-18 years old, who were there for something as simple as stealing a loaf of bread for their hungry family. Some of their sentences were for as long as four years. The young men lined up and stood at attention as we entered. Who could have imagined that just a few short years ago that we would be in a Russian prison, passing out Bibles and telling these young men about Jesus! The room overflowed and by the end of our service, 30 teens accepted Christ as their savior. I will never be the same again. Their faces will forever be etched in the caverns of my mind. As I went to leave, a young boy approached me, with tears streaming down his face, and just hugged me and wouldn't let go. It was then that I realized my purpose for being in the prison; The Holy Spirit brought about a divine appointment. He spoke no English, and my Russian again was limited, but the words just began to pour out of my mouth and his, and for a few God-given minutes, we understood each other, and his life and mine were touched in only a way that God could do it.

On the way home, we had a Ukrainian style picnic, where I had my first piece of cake with garlic and salt covering it. Can you imagine expecting something sweet, and swallowing that combination? That will be my first and last venture into Ukrainian baking cuisine for a long time to come.

We just got back to our apartment and are locked out and have decided to do an impromptu concert in the middle of the apartments where there is a small park area. It is amazing what the strumming of a few guitars and the sound of 8 off key voices can bring about, because kids are coming from everywhere. Even in a frustrating situation, the Holy Spirit always has a plan, because a young girl from L'viv University just walked up and asked us if we could come to her school and address the students and answer their questions about God! A locked door has led to the unlocking of young minds hungry for God. What has amazed me the most about the young people here is their innocence. They have not been penetrated by the bad side of western culture. Here, it is much like America in the 1930's. And to think that just several years ago under Communism, they weren't allowed to mention God, and teachers had to sign a document stating their disbelief in God. Now, how ironic is it that in order for us to have gotten into the prison, we had to bribe the guards…not with money, but they asked for Bibles!

As time is going by so quickly, I sense more and more that we are here to help start a church, which we would develop a long term relationship with. Amazingly, I have found out that Taras and some youth in his church want to step out in faith and start a new church work. Actually, last night I shared with someone that I sensed a real calling on Taras's life to become a pastor. My friend said, "Then, why don't you tell him what you feel?" It just seemed awkward to tell a total stranger in another country what you felt that God was saying about him. This Holy Spirit gift stuff can be overwhelming at times, but when we trust God and use the gifts that He has given us, He supernaturally moves!

This morning at breakfast, without sounding ultra-spiritual, I told Taras that maybe God was calling him into the ministry. Much to my amazement, he looked at me and said that was his heart's desire, but he wasn't sure just how to begin. It was then that I clearly saw God's divine plan in us meeting and our future relationship. He related that they had the blessing of their pastor, and tomorrow night, I will be at that church. I can't wait! It is a good Pentecostal church, but rather structured and rigid, unlike Taras and his youth.

Monday April 19th…Easter in Ukraine is a five day experience filled with food, fellowship, and church services. Today was the final day of the Easter celebration. We spent most of the day in church listening to kid's choirs and other singing groups. I can't believe that I have been here one week. So much has happened; new relationships, both personal and church wise. Taras will hopefully be coming soon to visit, and somehow, I believe that his new work here in L'viv, will be key to penetrating the rest of Ukraine and even Western Europe.

Tuesday April 20th… Today, Taras took us to the site of the former Nazi concentration camp, here in L'viv where 500,000 Jews died… Actually many more would have died if they hadn't hid in the sewers underneath L'viv. Many survived by hiding out there for over two years! Sadly, at the end of the war, many Jews who survived, renounced their Judaism and took out Russian citizenship because of fear. After World War II, the Communists forced collective farming upon the peasant farmers, but many refused to give up their private farms. What followed was the holocaust revisited, for the Russian army moved in and starved to death seven million Ukrainians by causing an artificial famine to sweep through Ukraine. The Russian forces overwhelmed the small villages, breaking out windows and stealing any source of wood or other heating supply they could get their hands on. It got so bad that parents were killing their children for food, just to survive. I remember how my grandparents despised the Russians for what they had done to Polish and Ukrainian people alike during that man-made famine. If someone came to visit their home and spoke Russian, they had to step out onto the porch to speak.

I am beginning to get a much clearer understanding why I have come to Ukraine.

I am sitting here journaling my thoughts about what has happened, but even more so about what is going to happen. I do not understand this clearly, but I believe my being here is an answer to the prayers of my Ukrainian ancestors many years ago in this place. But there is something else very heavy on my heart; I am feeling very impressed that Taras's youngest brother, 11 year old Yuriy is supposed to come and live with our family as an exchange student. That would take a miracle, because we have had a string of young people living with our family and decided that it was time for a break, and the last thing my wife, Diana, said before I left was, "Don't bring back any kids!" Yuriy is a very mature young man, but why would his parents allow him to go to a foreign land with total strangers at the age of 11? The economy here is very bad. Yuriy had to stand in line for three hours today to buy us bread for dinner.

We just went to the bank to exchange dollars for Ukrainian currency or "coupons," but there was no money in the bank.

How strange! But even stranger is how we have to take showers. The water is only on between 6-9 am and 6-9 pm, so if we want a shower and are lucky enough to be home then and have the water hot, we can enjoy something that we just take for granted at home-namely smelling ok. Then of course, we must never forget to fill the bathtub and have a bucket ready for the toilet... Oh, one more thing; toilet tissue cannot be flushed down the toilet and must be neatly placed in a basket by the toilet. Boy, do I love this place!

Wednesday April 21ˢᵗ ...It is 11:37 pm, and we are worn out from another adventurous day in the land of "Oz." Actually, I made another language blunder that got us lost for five hours. Let me explain. We went to the mall, if you want to call it a mall. All the shelves were empty except for a can of tomatoes, a car battery, and one piece of women's clothing-hardly Macys. Well after walking for 3 miles or so, we were wiped out and any dreams of exotic Ukrainian gift buying had quickly faded, so we wanted to go back to the apartment. One of the young Ukrainian girls walking with us asked me, or so I thought, "Are you ready to walk home?" I replied that we were more than ready. Well, what she really asked me was if we wanted to walk downtown, another 4-5 miles and see the city. For them to walk 10 miles a day is nothing, because that is how they get around. But for us that was no picnic in the park. Now three hours later, we realized something was quite wrong. We didn't know much about road signs, but it was evident that we should have been home hours ago. Exasperated, with sweat running down her brow, the young lady looked at me and asked if I wanted to see more of the city. It was then that I realized my blunder. I turned to our team and said that I had made a rather "small" mistake in my communications with the girl. Thank God for His mercy and grace, otherwise my team would have sold me to the highest bidder! So we found the nearest trolley and headed back the opposite direction. At this point, I have been officially banned from opening my mouth and saying anything in Russian. Oh, let me comment on the trolley ride. Our trolley was so jammed that we were piled on top of one another, hanging on to the hand railings that ran across the top of the bus ceiling. I mention the railings because, the temperature and humidity were very high and half the trolley was filled with passengers whose arms were raised holding on to the railings. I might also add that to my knowledge, deodorant has yet to be introduced on a wide scale basis in Ukraine. This aromatic experience made the 10 mile hike seem like a blessing!

Thursday April 22nd...Five days till we leave. I am very sad. This place has so captivated me . It is not just my heritage that draws me, but the fresh calling on my life to be a small part of something very large happening in Ukraine spiritually.

Today has been another typical day with new challenges awaiting us. We have occasionally had a car to take us around, but the journey in a Russian Lada, is not like riding in a Ford or Chevy. To begin the trip today, we had to pump up the front tires and then had to use a screw driver to open the trunk and get out a spare for the flat tire on the back. Then we had to find a knife to open the broken door latch. Finally, any trip with a Lada always commences with four of us pushing the car a half block to get it up and running. Lada cars are pieces of junk!

We ended up speaking at the school today. Well, it just so happened that the professor was fluent in Spanish, and of course one of our team members mentioned that I spoke Spanish. That was years ago in college! Now I was not only trying to understand her Russian and Ukrainian, but she began to speak to me a mile a minute in Spanish. If my brain wasn't fried before, it certainly is now!

Taras's calling overwhelms me. What are you saying Lord? What am I supposed to do? I feel like I am helping to write a book that is about the birthing of a movement here in Ukraine.

Friday April 23rd ... (4 days till we leave). I learned a lot about Taras today. He was in the Russian military when he committed his life to Christ. He had been on his way to Chernobyl, the sight of the nuclear disaster in Ukraine, to help in the cleanup process. He knew from others that those who went there would not be coming back alive. He had already lost several friends due to radiation poisoning in Chernobyl. He was half way to the site when his commander told them that they should pray, which Taras had been doing-asking God to forgive him of his sins, as well as turn their caravan of troop transports around. Suddenly, there came across the radio a command to turn the convoy around and head back. That answered prayer, quite likely saved his life as well as the future calling that the Holy Spirit had for him.

I learned a lot today about my ethnicity. Much of Ukraine was controlled by the Austro-Hungarian Empire until 1939 when Poland occupied eastern Ukraine. But the western part, which includes Kiev, where quite likely my grandparents were born, was under Russian control. So on my mom's side; I am a real mutt- Russian, ethnically Ukrainian and a little Polish tossed in for good measure!

Saturday April 23rd (3 days until we leave)…Spent most of the day hitchhiking all over L'viv. Taras has been with us all day…His poor wife…We keep running into a kid named Victor. I always see him coming over the sea of heads, because when I first got here, I gave him a Cleveland Indian's baseball cap, and he has never taken it off. I think that he sleeps with it. I wonder, why in a city of a million people, Victor keeps showing up. We are building a solid relationship. Sharing Christ is so simple. If we are listening and watching, He brings us opportunities and allows us to build our testimony into the lives of others. He can even use something as simple as a baseball cap!

Sunday April 25th (Two days until we leave)…Today, we covered all the Ukrainian church bases and what a contrast! This morning, we went to the Charismatic church and the worship service was very powerful. People were dancing in the isles, and the joy was amazingly overwhelming. The worship just exploded and seemed to engulf the whole congregation. I will never forget this encounter, because these people having nothing economically compared to us, but yet they are overflowing with a spirit that I long to experience and receive.

Well, tonight service brought a real contrast. We attended a traditional Pentecostal church. The people were wonderful, while the worship was a bit more conservative to say the least. The choir director got upset because, while our American worship leader was singing "Shine Jesus Shine," he was moving a little bit too much, and the choir director accused him of dancing. My thoughts went back to the morning worship service, where this choir director would have probably called the police! Legalism-it doesn't matter what country or church, it rears its ugly head and tries to stifle the spirit and stop the move of God.

As I said, putting aside the "dancing episode," this church has carried the message of Christ's saving Grace, even during the time of harsh rule under the Communists, and tonight, I was given the privilege of speaking from its historic pulpit. But it was not what I spoke that was so important, but what happened afterwards!

No sooner was I done speaking when Taras's father, Vladimir, came down the isle and put his arm around me and walked me to the door, speaking a mile a minute. Taras had spoken to his father about Yuriy coming to stay with my family, but there hadn't been a response. At the back door of the church, Vladimir continued to speak to me, and it was obvious that he was happy about something. Taras came over and joined the conversation. What happened next was so amazing that no words could describe what I felt! Vladimir simply said, after listening to me speak, that his son Yuriy could go with me any place in the world! Tomorrow, I will meet with Yuri's mother, Steffa, and that could be the next challenge. I must share a final note on today's adventures. We were again locked out of our apartment, and it was very cold, but inside I was burning with the Spirit and the realization that I had truly heard from God concerning Yuriy. Well, God has a unique way of capping off a day's experience. Because, as we stood in the freezing cold, a drunken man walked up and started fighting with anyone who looked at him cross-eyed. So here we are, in a foreign country, in freezing temperatures, locked out of our apartment, and dealing with an angry drunk. As he began to cross the apartment parking lot approaching us, I had visions of an old-fashioned brawl and ending up in some Ukrainian jail for five years for disorderly conduct. Somehow, this didn't seem like a divine appointment that I necessarily wanted to experience! Suddenly, out of nowhere, appeared a security guard who let us into the apartment complex to wait for our friends. Just when I thought that all of those "Rocky and Rambo" movie experiences might come in handy, our near rumble was over.

Monday April 26th (We leave tomorrow)... Today, I again ran into Victor, still wearing his "Chief Wahoo" baseball cap. The best way to describe him is that he is like a "needle in a hay stack" that somehow always turns up. We talked with him and said, "Goodbye," and gave him some money. I believe that I may not see the fruit of his life, but deep seeds have been planted. That is the true joy and purpose of divine appointments.

Tonight, I spoke to a youth group, and we had a tremendous ministry time. If nothing else has happened to me on this trip, one thing I know for sure; I am not going home the same. Whether I become a pastor- missionary or not, I am taking home, buried deep within my spirit, a mandate to be part of shaping Ukraine's future by helping to mentor a new generation of leaders that it might again experience the freedom to worship, which had been stolen from them by the Socialists and Communists. God is going to use our church to help spearhead that revolution and that will be the greatest divine appointment of all!

It is hard to say, "Goodbye," but I know that it is just the beginning of a wonderful journey that God has so blessed me *to take. By the way, Steffa, with many tears rolling down her face, said, "Yes," concerning Yuriys coming to America. Now, how do I explain to my three children that they have a new brother for one year, and my wife that she has a new son? Only God can work this one out!*

Tuesday April 27th ...We have left L'viv and taken the long train ride to Kiev, where we will fly out of to New York.

We had an uneventful night, except for the drunks singing. Taras has taken the trip with us to be sure that we get on the plane safely. After all that has spiritually happened on this trip, I haven't even thought about flying 9 hours home. Boy have I changed! Taras and I talked much of the night. I know that I have heard from God, and our relationship will be for a lifetime. We will be in Kiev until Thursday and begin the trek home.

Friday April 30th...Well, we have completed the long trek back to the States and have arrived at the airport in New York. As I sit here in Kennedy waiting for our connecting flight home, how can I even prepare my thoughts to share with my family and church? We have been traveling for 27 hours with all the stops, but it seems that I just left L'viv moments ago; probably because part of my heart never left. If I can now summarize a strategy, it would consist of getting Taras here to meet our church and to develop a plan to help him with his church planting. Secondly, my prayer is to see God work a miracle in bringing Yuriy here as an exchange student to help teach me Ukrainian.

There is so much more, but as I conclude my thoughts, I will wait on the Holy Spirit to take this vision and give it wings. After all, that is what divine appointments are for; to take jars of clay and transform them into anointed and spirit filled vessels of honor that He might be glorified as we are transformed into His likeness as vessels filled with His presence.

Lord, thank you for considering me worthy enough to have experienced these last two weeks. It is only by your grace that you would take a "home-boy" like me out of my comfort zone and begin an adventure that will consume my journey for the rest of my life to places yet unknown ruining my sometimes boring and ordinary life forever!

The faithfulness of God

The events which you have just read occurred in April 1993. Now, I want to fast forward to October 2010. Since that initial trip, which opened my eyes to the Apostolic calling on my life, I have traveled to Israel nine times and also to India, Armenia, Cyprus, most of the Middle East, Australia, and much of Europe. Back in 1993, I would never have dreamed of such an adventurous life and only by the power of the Holy Spirit, has it even come about!

However, what has been the greatest blessing, is seeing His Word fulfilled and multiplied! Taras became a pastor and now pastors "Bethesda Church" in L'viv, numbering 500 or more. Oh, and by the way, when I got home and was greeted by my wife, some amazing words came out of her mouth. She began, "This is not just a one-time trip for you to Ukraine, is it?" I responded that I sensed a deep calling to go back. Diana then responded that if that were so, we should pray for someone to live with us for a while to teach me the language. I was speechless to say the least. I simply replied that I totally agreed and that he was arriving in a few weeks!

Yuriy came to live with our family at the ripe old age of 11, and not only stayed for one year, but he came back for a second! While barely able to speak English, he managed to attain a 4.0 grade average. And by the way, we never had one Ukrainian language lesson during those two years!

Today, Yuriy has just graduated from medical school in Ukraine and handles our medical outreach teams that go to Bethesda Church to bring healing both physically and spiritually. He has married a wonderful girl named Marta who is a dentist and helps with our dental outreach. Yuriy has become, to the Glory of God, like his brother Taras, a bright and shining light in dark places. Often times divine appointments don't really seem divine until years have passed and the fruit is evident. All that the Holy Spirit is looking for is a willing heart; not one seeking personal glory, but a heart that is willing to help establish His kingdom rule and reign in the hearts of others, that His Glory might be revealed. Thank you, Holy Spirit, that what you promise and reveal, you are faithful to fulfill!

Chapter 2

Let Your Heart Be Your Guide

"It is when we tackle the unknown that often times
the future is revealed."

My Ukrainian odyssey was now behind me, but a new challenge was about to hit me right between the eyes. Jacob and Jaya were missionaries from South India whom I had met through an incredible set of circumstances. They had been attending our church for a number of years, and in fact, we had helped to establish one of Jacob's children's homes in Sitarampuram, South India, a household word that I am sure is common to most of you. But beyond his missionary work in his homeland of India, Jacob had one goal in mind; getting me to India! I cannot begin to recount how many times I heard, "Pastor, until you go, the people will never understand, and you will never know the meaning of taking the Gospel to other nations." I had been called out of more than one church service and told that I had an apostolic calling to the nations on my life, but I didn't understand the vast spiritual implications of those words. Apostolic calling—I didn't know what the word actually meant in the context of being used, but I had an idea that it had something to do with airplanes and overseas traveling; two things that I wanted no part of! But, the Holy Spirit has a way of turning our fears into fantastic adventures with Him, when we allow our hearts to govern our actions, as I was about to find out.

Sunday morning service was about to begin when Jacob Beera approached me. I knew what was coming, for Jacob and his wife Jaya were preparing to return to their mission work in Southern India. I had met Jacob in 1978 through a routine appointment for mission support, but the Holy Spirit had much more in mind, and we had become instant friends and partners in ministry. Yet, Jacob had not been able to convince me to go to India with him. Every year about this time, Jacob would challenge me to go with him to see the children's homes being established there, as well as the tremendous outreach to new Hindu converts. We had supported the building of High Mill Children's Home in Sitarampuram, a small village in south India and were now supporting the children and missionary work there. My argument was always the same; "I believe that missions begin at home, and God knows that we have enough work to do here!" Yet, I knew as well as Jacob that those words were simply excuses, because I did not like flying and could not imagine being separated from my family so far from home for a whole month.

As Jacob came closer, I had my canned answer ready; "Not this year but maybe next." As I prepared to respond, Jacob looked at me with those dark brown and piercing Indian eyes and said, "Chuck, if you never go, how will the church ever understand the importance of missions?" As I began to tremble, he asked me again, "Will you go with us this January?" Without hesitating, I responded with a big, "Yes, I will go!" As I sat down waiting for the service to begin, my wife asked me just how I had gotten out of going this time. When I told her that I had said yes, she responded that I had made the right decision and it was time. Well, after her comment, I knew that my life was about to take an exciting turn! It wasn't like I was going an hour's distance to Cleveland to watch the Indians play baseball, but my three day trek, by plane, train, and God knows what else would take me to the other side of the world and would open my heart to new and exciting divine appointments.

Sitarampuram, Mori, Vizag, and Eluru; these were the names of places that I had never heard of, but would become commonplace as we traveled to visit the children's homes that Jacob had established.

After the 24 hour plane flight, and 8 hour train ride, we arrived at our destination in Mori, and soon enough, would be introduced to some new and interesting challenges.

As I think back to the many lessons that God taught me during my India stay, one in particular stands out; I learned to be thankful for each day that I was alive and still breathing. Let me explain. Indian drivers are like none that I have ever seen. Their daring way is only superseded by their counterparts in Damascus, Syria. Often times we would drive at night with neither head light working, and what made matters worse, we would face on-coming vehicles driving at excessive speeds with their head lights burned out also; sometimes on one lane roads! One day we were driving on a narrow lane in the middle of nowhere and came to a bend that was not wide enough for two cars to pass. You guessed it; as we approached the bend, a truck filled with 20 Indian men met us head-on. Because there was no room to back up or turn around, we were at a real stalemate! Our driver, who was built like a middle line-backer/tight end, got out of our van and began to challenge the truck driver demanding that he back up and let us by. My first reaction was that he knew something that I didn't, like an imminent US missile strike taking place if they didn't comply or something else just as farfetched. Outnumbering us twenty to six, they were not about to do any such thing, and when 10 of them jumped off the truck, I began to thank the Lord for a long and wonderful life. After about five minutes of screaming and finger pointing, I turned to Jacob and asked him what they were yelling about. He simply said that they did not like us very much. Whether it was the size of our driver or the Holy Spirit, I don't know, but suddenly all 10 men jumped back on the truck and their driver slowly and very carefully, backed down the mountain road so that we could pass. When that episode was over, Jacob just turned to me and said, "Welcome to India!"

One more Indian road trip adventure deserves to be mentioned, because it was an experience that will forever be part of my fond memories of India. We had been traveling to another village and had been on the road for a short time when we came to a bridge. It wasn't just any bridge, because it towered several hundred feet over a dry riverbed that only contained water during the monsoon season. The bridge was made out of wood and seemed to sway in the Indian breeze. I remember thinking that it had to be at least 100 years old, and I wasn't far off. As we began to cross, we came to a red light and had to stop approximately 400 feet out onto the bridge. It was then that I realized that it was a one lane bridge and there was traffic directly across facing us. I looked to my right and left and realized very quickly that a driver would have to be a Houdini to get passed us. We sat there for 10 minutes waiting for what, I did not know. Then slowly a long lane of oncoming trucks and buses began to move towards us. These weren't small vehicles but large trucks and buses carrying a lot of weight. As each additional vehicle entered onto the bridge, the swaying increased dramatically. We just sat there as the vehicles somehow squeezed by our lane of traffic, occasionally bumping vehicles in front and behind us. I remember looking down to the riverbed and thinking to myself, no one would ever believe this story. Then suddenly, my eye caught a rather large piece of wood falling off the bridge and crashing below. Then another piece fell off. It seemed that with the weight of each new vehicle entering on to the bridge, debris was falling from everywhere. I turned to Jacob and asked him how old the bridge was. "Don't worry," he said, "The British built it in 1886 and guaranteed it for 100 years." Wow, that seemed to make things better, until my amazing mathematics background kicked in and I realized that this being 1994, the bridge was 107 years old! I said, "Jacob, this bridge is way past 100 years old, so when are they going to build a new one?" Jacob looked at me and smiled saying, "They will build a new one when this one falls down." Wow, that made me feel so much better considering we were 200 feet in the air and swaying in the wind with chunks of our British built bridge falling to the riverbed below! You might be interested in knowing that in 2006, Indian contractors finally built the new one, and yes, the old one made it to the very end!

A short time after our arrival, I was invited to participate in a baptismal service at an outdoor canal. I was really excited and blessed to be asked. It was an honor to witness such an event, because for an Indian, who had been a Hindu, to give his life to Christ and enter the waters of baptism, meant that he or she could lose his family, career, job, and yes, even his life. My excitement began to ebb when we reached the canal, and I realized that the canal was not only used for baptism but was used to wash clothes, as well as water buffalo. Not only that, but it was used for human waste and was the only source of drinking water for that village! In short, it was an open sewer...Occasionally dead bodies could be seen floating down the canal waters. I turned to Jacob and said that I felt a strong leading of the Holy Spirit to video the service and not help baptize. He looked at me and laughed, because he knew that my body, save a miracle from the Holy Spirit, did not have immunities to deal with what was in the water. So I videotaped but almost found it impossible to see through the tears, as I heard stories of faith and persecution that were beyond words. This divine appointment at the canal was for me, because it grew my faith in ways that were right out of the pages of the New Testament.

I could relate many more amazing stories and travel adventures during my stay in India, but it was my initial trip from the train station to the village that I will always remember. Most Indian villages have huge canals that run through them, and where, as stated, they receive their drinking water, wash their water buffalos, and use them for garbage and bathrooms. On this first night, our van driver took us on a one-lane road that actually split the canal in half. That would have been ok except every fifty feet or so, we were passing another vehicle or animal drawn carriage. In order to pass, the driver would literally have one side of the van tilting no more than a foot from the road's edge. I remember looking out my window at the twenty-foot deep canal which was only a few moments and inches away from swallowing up our van and confessing any sins that still might be lingering in my life. But I might add, after three weeks of traveling that one lane dirt road every day, I came to have full trust in our driver, whom I determined had an anointing from God like few drivers I had ever known.

Maybe because it was just my second mission trip, but India seemed to offer a thrill a day. Late the next afternoon, we had settled into our rooms and were getting this India "thing" down pretty good, when our next adventure took place. Jacob brought us in a case of Indian pop minus refrigeration and ice. It was so hot that even warm pop seemed satisfying. As we were searching for a can opener, I turned to one of our team members and questioned where Limca and Goldspot (Indian brand names), might be bottled. I jokingly said that I hoped that no mice got into the bottles before they were filled with pop. Just then, I looked over as one team member was about to chug down a Limca. To my amazement, I noticed a brown mass at the bottom of the bottle. I screamed, "Don't drink that!" Well, you guessed it. Lodged in the bottle's bottom was a dead mouse. It took several days before we could even look at pop, but due to the heat and thirst, soon gave in. Thankfully, we never had that Indian mouse experience again!

For those of you who have a passionate love for large furry spiders, I have one more tale to tell. I awakened one morning and was about to leave for the shower several buildings away, when I glanced at the table near the door and saw what seemed to be an eight inch wide hairy spider just staring at me. Anyone who knows me understands my love for such creatures, especially big hairy ones! For the next 20 minutes, I plotted my escape but didn't have much success. It didn't help that the night before, I watched dinosaur-like lizards crawling out of holes in my ceiling. And the fact that their eyes glowed in the dark didn't help matters. I had told Jaya about them, and her response was not to worry if they were green (which they were), but if they were brown, after one bite, I would have no more than a minute and a half to live. That deeply reassured me. Well, back to my spider friend. I managed to get the door open, and much to my amazement, a gust of wind knocked him off the table and onto the floor. It was then that I realized that it was only a spider skin and not a real live one. I ran next door to tell several of my team members about my near death experience, and they seemed to be deeply concerned about my well-being.

That night, we were speaking under a giant Pandal (an Indian tent covered with palms). There were at least three thousand people gathered for the service. But when it came time for me to speak, something surreal began to happen. My interpreter, while introducing me began to slowly walk across the stage in a crouched position. It was as if he was being very fearful and cautious at the same time. Then he began to point at me, and the crowd began to roar. In my life I had been laughed at for many things but never 14,000 miles from home and in a language that I had never heard! Now, I was being laughed at by 3,000 Indians!

Suddenly it hit me. It had to do with that spider. The Interpreter was mimicking me trying to get out of my room. It was then that my team members, who were on stage with me, began to laugh uncontrollably. I don't know who was laughing louder, the 3,000 Indians or my so-called friends, because, it was a team member who had placed the spider on my table without me knowing it. It was all they could do that day to not collapse in laughter as they told person after person about my near death adventure!

One of the most difficult things for me involving traveling was leaving my family. It is a very helpless feeling to be over 10,000 miles from home with nothing more to communicate with than a rickety old phone that worked certain hours and only if the power was on.

It was early one evening, and we were preparing for the first night of the rally under the Pandal. People were traveling from many miles away to hear the Gospel preached by sea-soned Indian teachers and evangelists. My first reaction was one of intimidation; what was I doing on this stage with so many gifted speakers? That coupled with a sense of fear from being so far from my family, caused panic to rise in my heart and emotions. I quietly cried out to God that He had gotten me here, and now I needed His assurance that everything would be ok.

God often answers our prayers in unique and strange ways. This night was to be no different. As the worship was about to begin, a middle-aged man walked up to Jacob, the mission's head, and asked if he could sing a song. Well, every church has one or two well-meaning individuals who have a way of wanting to say or do things, with the right motive, but at the wrong time. Jacob kindly told him that worship was begin-ning and there was no time for him to sing. He seemed to understand and turned to leave the stage. But before he left, he walked over to me and handed me a sheet of paper with a picture of me and our team. Above my picture was scrawled Genesis 28:15. The local church had passed out fliers with our pictures and advertisements about our being guest speakers. I was about to discard the paper, not realizing that I quite likely was in the presence of one of those "angels unaware" the Bible talks about. Then the scripture seemed to jump out at me, and I picked up my Bible to read it. The date was January 16th 1994; a date that I would never forget. Because that day, for me, would become a day of liberation from fear concerning the calling on my life involving missions. No longer would fear and worry grip my heart about my family's safety, nor would concern about being away from my church rob me any longer of God's blessing.

It might seem too simple to the average reader, but what was logos for some became rhema to me. "And behold, I am with you and will keep watch over you with care. I will take notice of you wherever you may go, and I will bring you back to this land; for I will not leave you until I have done all of which I have told you." God's promise to Jacob in Genesis 28:15, had become my promise from God that He was in charge, and all that I needed to do was trust. An angel, a divine appointment, or maybe just an accident, all I know is that the Holy Spirit used a materially poor Indian man to bless me with the riches of the Kingdom and release me into a whole new realm of ministry, as well as releasing me to the nations. From that night at the Pandal, my life began to immediately change. No longer was my focus on the things that worried me but on what He now was ready to do in and through me. Soon, I began to experience His divine presence as I had never seen before.

It was during the initial crusade meetings at the Pandal that my faith in God's healing power would be strengthened. During these yearly crusades, people came from many miles away, often through word of mouth about the wonderful things that Jesus was doing and had done. The church and crusade team didn't need any ad campaign or public relations firm to get the word out. All they had was the Holy Spirit, and He was doing a fine job, thank you!

I believe that it was one of the first nights of the crusade, and speakers had been preaching since about 1:00 pm, and it was now 7:00 pm. After one Indian evangelist ended, Jacob went to the microphone and asked if anyone needed prayer for healing, to please come to the front. In most American churches, when such a call is given, a few people will meander down, and the trickle will continue for 10 or 15 minutes. Well, India was quite a different story. Immediately hundreds out of the crowd of three to four thousand rushed to the front pinning our team against the wall. It happened so quickly that I didn't have time to move away from the surging crowd. I had never seen people so hungry for prayer. They began to kiss our feet and touch our clothing as if there was something holy about us. Immediately, we began to point towards heaven telling them that it was Jesus and not us. Only He had the power to heal and set people free! Because most of them spoke little English, it was very difficult to get them to understand.

The very first man, who came to me for prayer, grabbed my left hand and thrust it into his thigh. Much to my chagrin, my hand seemed to disappear deep into his flesh. I looked down and realized that my fingers were actually touching his bone. The man had a terrible infection that had eaten away the flesh, and all that remained was a gaping hole. At that point, I nearly passed out and at the same time began thanking God for the handi-wipes that I had placed in my pocket. The prayer continued for hours, and many other tragic situations gripped our hearts, but in the midst of the emotional pain and suffering, Jesus let us know that He was still in charge.

As I was praying for someone, the crowd was surging around our severely outnumbered team. Then to my right, I heard a lady begin to shout. Her voice seemed to lift above the noise around me. I soon realized that something incredible was taking place, but I couldn't get a good look. Finally, I turned to Jacob and asked him what was going on. In a very matter of fact way, he responded that she had just seen her husband and children for the first time. "Where have they been," I asked? "They haven't been anywhere; you see, Chuck, she has been blind since birth, and God just opened her eyes!" I just stood there in amazement, watching that little lady jump up and down. If she was only acting out her joy, then she deserved an Oscar.

It was early one morning, when Jacob came to me and said that he had received a message from a family in another village. Their mother was nearly dead, and they wondered if Jacob would come and pray with her and the family. When he asked me to go, I immediately said yes. We got into a very primitive canoe and headed down the river. I will never forget the canoe, because the water was within inches of the canoe's edge, and there were strange looking neon like glowing fish just staring at us along side of the boat.

We reached the hospital where the family had gathered around the bed of the lady who had been in a deep coma since November, and it was now January. She had been diagnosed as having a stroke but, like the hospital, the treatment and medical care were primitive to say the least, so no one really knew the reason for her coma. But one thing was for sure; her stare was fixed and had been for a long time, and her body was very stiff and lacked any color.

Jacob placed his hand upon her forehead and began to pray for God the Holy Spirit to divinely intercede and heal the woman. He continued to pray for some time. He stopped and then prayed a second time. After waiting a few moments, he prayed a third time, but the lady remained motionless. Jacob turned to me and said that we had done all that we could do and it was time to leave. As the family continued to mourn, we turned to go, when something happened that I will never forget. The hospital was no more than a few bamboo huts strung together with very little room for a bed. I remember how stifling the heat was, and so as we were about to walk out of the door, I was grateful for the cold burst of air that hit me in the face. My first thought was, "Thank God for the air conditioner coming on!" But just as quickly, I realized that this simple Indian hospital didn't have air conditioning! As a matter of fact, they had never seen such a modern day marvel! And what's more, there was very little electricity in the village. And then it happened again. It was as if I had walked into a refrigerator room where meat would be kept. I turned back towards Jacob, and with a big grin, he said, "We need to pray some more!" No words could ever explain what happened next. As Jacob prayed again, that lady's chest began to move with breathing that was much deeper than before. Family members began to scream, and being nominal believers at best, were overwhelmed with the healing presence of Jesus. Then someone pulled back the sheets exposing her legs, which began to move. Before my eyes, those legs, which had resembled pieces of dead wood suddenly began to soften and gain color. People began to run out of the room and into the village proclaiming what God had done. Then, Jacob turned to me and said that it was time to go, and that God was finished with us. Go? How could we just go? The third part of the Holy Trinity had just shown up and healed a lady who was about to die and we were just going to leave. One week later, this story would take an even greater turn. Jacob had to go back to that particular village and asked if I wanted to go. Of course I said that I wanted to, because part of the trip's purpose was to revisit the hospital and check on the little old lady. With expectancy and joy, we walked into the hospital room and there she was, sitting on the edge of the bed dangling her feet over the edge. She was being released and about to go home! News of her marvelous healing spread throughout the surrounding villages to such an extent that revival broke out. I would come to learn before my Indian experience would end that such experiences were common and not only common, but expected!

I could relate so many more divine appointments, but they would occupy the rest of this book. So I will close this chapter of my life with one short one. Each night, a young boy would show up at the crusade pulling himself along with a stake. He was paralyzed from the waist down and, each night was making the trip from several miles away. For some reason, my heart just broke for him and his circumstances. I wanted to do something, but what? All I could offer was prayer, but at that point, the Holy Spirit had not chosen to touch him physically.

My three weeks in South East India soon came to a close; so many stories, so many miracles, and yes, so much spiritual growth. Yet, as I prepared to leave, that young boy's face seemed to always occupy center stage in my mind, and so I continued to pray that God would answer his faithfulness for showing up every night at the Pandal. I would later receive an answer to my prayers.

One year later, Jacob and Jaya returned from their yearly trip, and we were having lunch. Then my memory went back to our previous years' experience. "Whatever happened to that young boy who crawled to the meetings on a stake?" "Well, I have great news," Jacob responded. "He came back again this year, and God instantly healed his paralyzed limbs!" I was speechless! "Why now and not then?" Many other thoughts and feelings flooded my mind, but one thing was for sure; I now felt like my odyssey in India had closure and a very blessed trip was now complete!

Chapter 3

The God of Great Surprises

"Happiness is a poor substitute for joy, because happiness is borne out of chance, while joy is a daily expression of His presence surprising us with new adventures."

M y experiences in India had wondrously built my faith, but even more so, had prepared me for new and exciting experiences in a part of the world that I never dreamed that I would go.

1994 began as one of the hardest years of my life. Actually, the previous year had not been much better. My mom had gotten progressively sicker and eventually would be diagnosed with terminal cancer, and within our church, divisions sprung up which put more stress on our family and marriage. I had come to view the "valley of the shadow" which David talked about in Psalms 23 in a realistic manner. The Hebrew understanding meant more than just physical death, but also the everyday experiences that make up the struggles of life and living. Yet the reality of Jesus' love and care and the fact that He had blessed us with three marvelous children, kept our joy before us. After all, compared to many others, we were truly blessed and knew it. But that still didn't make the pain and stress any less easy to deal with. Our existence seemed to revolve around just making it to the next day. Have you ever been there? It is where any forward thinking or vision casting seems so farfetched, because just dealing with people, issues, problems, and division makes any future hope seem highly improbable.

It was early one afternoon, and there was a knock on my office door. Not wanting to deal with another problem, I really didn't want to open it. But when I did, standing there was a very trusted friend and intercessor whose prayers had seen me through many a hard time. "I have something for you," she began. Well that meant that sometime during the night, God had given her a "word" for me. During a time when God seemed to be speaking directly to so many self-proclaimed prophets, (by the way, according to Old Testament rules concerning prophesy, being wrong could be hazardous to your health), I was highly skeptical of anyone who invoked the name of the Almighty and seemed to speak for Him, knowing all the mysteries of the kingdom. But I was not skeptical of this young lady. Cheryl spoke with authority and integrity about the things that God had given her, and when she spoke, I listened!

She began by telling me that she had been praying for me and my family. She continued that she knew that we and the church were under direct assault, but that the Holy Spirit would make a way for us to escape for a season and be restored and that God would see our church through these troubled waters. I told her thank you and that I would relish a time of healing and restoration, but in my heart knew that such a thing seemed impossible for the moment. Then she preceded to hand me two pieces of paper with a "word" for my wife and I. What followed was a true odyssey and example of God's care and love in the worst of times and seasons, for her word would not only lead to one of the most incredible divine appointment experiences of my life but open my heart for a land that I never cared to visit and a vision for ministry that I never dared to imagine. She had carefully typed out what the Holy Spirit had given her.

"Chuck, I had a vision of an airplane which would travel a far distance...This vision had to do with you and Diana. You will need to take a rest. You will choose a place to go which won't be too far. Your decision will be based on affordability. The Lord will provide a better place. He will provide the way for it to be available for you. The place I saw was a tropical place with trees like palm trees. The scenery was much like that of Hawaii. When you arrive at this place, you will have such peace, and it will be so fulfilling and relaxing for you both. I saw Diana being literally served by others. She was sitting there having everything she needed being provided for her. Her food was even brought to her and fed to her. You were not concerned for your children, for they were being well taken care of. You knew that your children were very content in where they were staying and with whom they were staying. The peace you and Diana were experiencing was a peace that you have not experienced before. It will be the peace of God; the peace that surpasses all understanding. There will be a time of rest for you. That rest time will be provided by the Lord for you... "Peace I leave with you; my peace I give to you...not as the world gives do I give to you. Let not your heart be troubled, nor let it be fearful..." John 14:27

As I listened to Cheryl, I thought, "This is just like God... Here I am feeling totally overwhelmed, and God sends a young lady to tell me that I am going on a vacation, to a place that I have apparently never been nor ever considered going to." Well, I took her words home and placed them in a drawer where no one could find them...If this was God, we had to know beyond any doubt without anyone making it happen. Our answer would come very soon.

A close friend in the church, who understood our struggles, asked me out for lunch a few days later. As we finished lunch, he asked me one of those questions that you know has a lot more behind it than the asking. He began, "Where are you and your family going to get away this summer? Do you have a vacation spot in mind?" My first reaction and thought was, "Vacation?" I was praying just to make it to tomorrow and somehow, that thought didn't have the word vacation in it. Then suddenly, remembering Cheryl's word, I began to shake inside. I asked him just why he had asked me that question when I obviously needed to remain at church and deal with the division and strife. He got a reassuring smile on his face and responded that the problems will still be there whether I am gone for a few weeks or not. And, I needed a break as well as my family. I liked the sound of his logic more every minute. Then he revealed the reason for his asking. "If you don't have any place to go this summer, I and my family would love to have you come with us to Israel." I remember feeling like I had just been dunked in a vat of ice water. Suddenly so many questions began swirling in my mind, with every one being an excuse why we couldn't go. We could never afford it, and we could never leave our three kids that long. I had never considered going to Israel and never would have dreamed that someday, I would be part of a youth ministry working in Israel. I'll share more about another amazing divine appointment in Israel later. Little did I realize that this divine appointment was a door to walk through, which would change the rest of my life.

Suddenly, my mind went back to Cheryl's word, and it all was beginning to come together. "Phil," I began, "Tell me about the topography of the land and the places that we will be going to." Before he could answer, I asked him a very important question. "Are there any really tropical places in Israel?" "Why do you ask?" He replied. Not knowing about Cheryl's word concerning us flying to a tropical place like Hawaii, he had no idea just why that was so important to me. He looked at me and began to smile. "Well, that is part of the surprise." Surprise? What surprise? "If you want to know, we are going to stay a few days in Eilat which is south of the Dead Sea and near the Egyptian border. Eilat is one of the truly tropical spots in the nation of Israel and we are staying at a fabulous resort called the Princess Hotel." Suddenly, it was as if I was living out an incredible dream. Cheryl's Word began to match Phil's words. We would go to a place of rest and receive healing.

Words could never describe the beauty of South Israel and the Princess Hotel. The browns and grays of the surrounding barren mountains cascaded down to the white sandy beaches which gave way to crystal clear waters overlaying the deepest emerald blue stone that I had ever seen. For miles and miles, the shimmering blue waves rose up to meet the deep blue Israeli sky. No place had ever offered me more peace and rest.

Well, how could we afford such a trip and what about our three children? True to the Word given us by Cheryl, Phil let me know that all expenses, except food would be covered and all three children were going too! Amazingly, a day later, Phil called to let me know that he and his wife Thelma wanted to cover the food expenses also. I was truly at a loss for words and totally humbled at the same time. Not only had the trip become affordable, (you can't top an all-expense paid trip to Israel for five people), but our kids were going with us!

God is so awesome! When we got to the hotel and realized how much it cost per person per day, we realized how much had been sacrificed for our well-being and rest. How ironic that Cheryl had said that my wife would be treated like royalty, and there we were in the Princess Hotel truly being treated like a king and princess! But God had one more surprise divine appointment awaiting us.

Early the next morning, with news about some peace treaty and border openings between Israel and Jordan filling the local news, we had the untold joy of sailing on the Bay of Aqaba on a beautiful yacht. Our kids, along with Phil and Thelma's, were soon in the warm waters splashing around. My thoughts immediately went to sharks, but I was assured that no sharks had been seen in those waters for over 20 years. How interesting, that we were only home a few weeks when I watched a news special on a recent shark attack in the Bay of Aqaba right where we had been swimming! Anyways, after about an hour or so in the hot Israeli sun, we were thinking about going back to shore when several TV helicopters began to circle our yacht, with another no more than several hundred yards away. We had no idea what was going on except that we were being filmed by Israeli TV cameras.

It was only after we had reached shore that we realized what all the commotion was about. We had just been eyewitnesses to history being made and didn't know it. On the yacht that had been a short distance away, sat the delegations from Israel and Jordan hammering out the final details for peace between Israel and Jordan. This very important meeting between the two former enemies was happening right before our eyes! Here, at Ein Aurona, on July 18th and 19th 1994, located just inside the boundary area north of Aqaba and Eilat, peace was being made! The delegate's efforts would lead to King Hussein of Jordan and Prime Minister Rabin of Israel signing "The Washington Declaration," at the White House on July 25th, with President Clinton as witness. A final "Treaty of Peace" would be signed on October 26th between Israel and Jordan. This truly was a place of Peace, where peace was being made! I could only stand and marvel at Cheryl's word and God's amazing grace. How can I ever forget my first odyssey in Israel? Little did I realize that my introduction to the land of Abraham, Isaac, and David was only the beginning of an adventure that would continue for a lifetime!

Chapter 4

Souled Out

"Many people walk in and out of your life, but true friends
leave footprints on your heart."
Eleanor Roosevelt

Our time in Israel with our friends from church had been
amazing. From Jerusalem to En Gedi, from Masada
to the Dead Sea, and from the Sea of Galilee to the Golan
Heights, we had a crash course in Middle Eastern history and
religion. How could we ever forget Bethlehem and Nazareth,
Jericho and Yad Hashmona, as well as being baptized in the
Jordan River? With many of these experiences behind us, we
were mentally getting prepared to leave a vacation and visit
of a lifetime. But God hadn't brought us all this way without
more in mind, because we were about to meet a couple who's
calling and mission would propel us to a more passionate love
for the land of Israel and her people.

It was early in the afternoon, and the hot Israeli sun was
almost too much to bear. As we were sitting by the pool at the
Ramot hotel, a short walking distance from the Sea of Galilee,
we noticed a rather large group of teenagers at the other end
of the pool being rather rowdy and loud. We immediately sur-
mised that they had to be Americans. My wife Diana, who usu-

ally wasn't comfortable meeting new people and especially rowdy ones like these, got up from the table and said that she was going over to meet them and their apparent chaperones and leaders. Well no sooner had she left, when she returned with the leaders for me to meet. That was my first encounter with Ed and Cathy, and it would begin a relationship that would span two states, two ministries, and a lifetime!

As we began to share, we couldn't talk fast enough. And our words kept tumbling over each other's words, but it didn't matter. We instantly realized that something special was happening, and that God had divinely brought us together! We both had been involved in working with youth. While we pastured a young church, Ed and Cathy were leading a growing youth movement in Arlington Heights Illinois, just outside of Chicago. Ed's love for sports mirrored mine, except that he rooted for the wrong teams like Da Bulls and White Sox for starters. But I soon learned to look past his wrong sport's loyalties to his heart of gold and love for all youth, especially Israeli and Arab. Ed was sort of a crazy guy, I couldn't help but think. He wore "biker leathers" and bandannas and rode Harleys, but could sure relate to kids. Cathy was an amazing story in her own right. It seemed like she was the "mom" to many of the fifty or so teens with them, and I very quickly saw her heart and compassion. As we began to talk about our backgrounds, we suddenly realized that we had attended the same seminary in Southern California at the same time and had been impacted by the same mentors and teachers! Only God would take two couples from different states and have them meet half way around the world to bind their hearts together in ministry and love. We left the Galilee with not only incredible memories but new friends who would play an important role in our journey of faith.

We were only home several weeks, when we found ourselves heading for Chicago to do a youth retreat in Ed and Cathy's home, which had really become a half-way house for many troubled teens. Ed and Cathy, affectionately known as "Mister Ed and Mrs. B," were at a cross roads in their ministry. They had taken teens to Israel for several years but now sensed a higher and more intensive calling to Israel. I will never forget the Saturday evening service. After a lot of worship and testimonies, we placed Cathy in the center of the circle and began to pray for God's will for their lives and ministry. Ed had not been there for the beginning, but when he entered the room, we placed him in the center and began to pray for him also.

That night, "Souled Out Ministries" was birthed. Actually the Lord had given Diana the name during the worship. Before long Heart and Soul Café with its loud music and amazing testimonies of God's saving love would be commissioned, ministering to hundreds of troubled teens every Saturday night.

How could I ever put into words the next five years? God allowed us to be part of Souled Out's ministry outreach to young people in Israel. The stories and divine appointments alone could fill the pages of this book! I will never forget one early Jerusalem evening when our dance team, made up of approximately 40-50 young people, were done performing and were beginning to mingle and talk with the Israeli youth who had gathered to listen to the music and observe the one hour performance, complete with lighting, smoke machines, and an excellent sound system. Suddenly one of our young people came and asked me to come and talk to a young Israeli girl who was on the ground bent over and crying uncontrollably. When I asked her what was wrong, her response overwhelmed me. She began by saying that the young girl that had come and gotten me, had just told her that there was someone who loved her unconditionally and could forgive her of all of her sins. Through her tears, she said, "Is that true? Can this Yeshua (Jesus) forgive me for all the terrible things that I have done?" She went on to share about her life and what she had experienced, including an abortion. But the most amazing part of our conversation was that she had never been told that anyone could love her that way, and that Yeshua had in fact died for her sins and could remove her guilt and shame. In fact, she had never heard His name before! On another warm

Israeli evening, on the beaches of Tel Aviv, our team had just ended their hour-long performance, when a young Arab boy approached a team member and seemed very excited. It took us a short time to find the right translators, but when we did, we found out that he was from Jordan and was visiting for one more day. He said that the meaning of the dances and the beauty of the songs had drawn him. After a brief conversation, he stated that he wanted to believe in this Yeshua (Jesus) that he had heard us sing about. Being a Jordanian Muslim, this was a dangerous step. We prayed together, and he simply left to go back to his room down the street, but for him, his night was just beginning. About the same time the next evening, our performance was over and there again was that young man. This time, he was even more emotional and begged to talk to anyone who would listen. We rounded up the interpreters and began to listen to a story that seemed to fall from the pages of the Bible. When he had gone home that previous evening, he had gone to bed and prayed, as we had asked him to do, that Yeshua would reveal Himself. He said that it was sometime in the middle of the night, that he was awakened by a brilliant light that filled his room. Out of the light came a voice; "I am Yeshua, the one that they have told you about. I am the way, the truth, and the life, and it is only through Me that you can know God the Father." The young boy had met Yeshua and would never be the same again! Now, he was both weeping and joyfully shouting at the same time! "I am going back to Amman, Jordan, a different person. I may lose my life, family, job, schooling, and friends, but to know Yeshua is more important to me than even life itself." We never saw him again, but I believe that today, some place in Jordan or the Middle East, there are a group of believers in Jesus Christ whose lives have been changed by one divine appointment that took place on a sandy beach in Tel Aviv.

There are many testimonies from my Souled Out adventures that I could relate, but there is one more that still grips my heart with the grace of God's mercy and love. Because of the intense heat during the day, for most Israelis, the day begins late into the evening. And usually around midnight, the cities really come to life. So it was one late Jerusalem evening when we found ourselves performing in one of the worst sections of Jerusalem. The stench of drugs and urine permeated the entire area. Yet a large crowd of youth had gathered to listen to the Christian rap and hip hop, as well as watch the performance. Because of the area that we were in and the danger of terrorism, our young people had dressed in civilian clothing and not their Souled Out t-shirts and so they somewhat blended in with the crowd. The performance ended, and hundreds of young people had stayed behind to talk with our kids about Yeshua. The scene was incredible; the plaza area where we had performed was filled with people weeping, praying, and rejoicing. It was approximately 1:30 am when suddenly a strong discernment and fear swept over me. I looked across the plaza and caught Cathy's eye and knew that she felt the same thing. Our youth were trained to take down our equipment and load the bus at a moment's notice. We had been able to do the loading in less than 5 minutes, and that was amazing when you considered all the speakers, key boards, guitars, and smoke machine. Immediately we signaled to our team that there was an emergency and we had to go…Now!! A few young people, who were praying with others at first balked, but when they realized just how serious Cathy and I were, they got the message. Within just a few minutes we were on our way not realizing the grave danger that was almost upon us.

It was only a matter of a week or so, and we were back in the States when an American pastor e-mailed me and told me about what had almost happened to us that early morning in downtown Jerusalem. He had been at the back of the crowd of 500-1000 and was located at a point that had not been visible to us. Suddenly, out of nowhere a mob had formed and was coming with stones to attack us. Their reasons were varied, but the biggest one was that we were singing about Jesus. The gentleman continued that then, as if on cue, you suddenly were gone in an instant! He said that God had really been looking out for us, because the mob was no more than five minutes from being on top of us! I learned an important lesson that night in that where God leads, He protects and provides. I also came to realize that the enemy hates God's divine timing, because many young people came to Jesus that night and not even a mob from hell could thwart God's divine appointment for their lives!

Being part of Souled Out allowed me to experience not only incredible relationships, but the Holy Land like few ever could. I had never considered going to the land of Israel, let alone being involved in ministry there, but what the Holy Spirit had in store, I could have never visualized. Birthed by a string of divine appointments, my destiny and legacy would now include a passion for other nations, beginning with Israel. Yes, five years and nine trips to the Holy Land would consummate in a deep love for the land, as well as a purposed heart for missions elsewhere.

As I look back over those years of ministry to youth all over Israel, it sometimes seems almost like a dream; a dream too big to comprehend. But isn't that like God? He challenges us to attempt the impossible and believe in the incredible. And when that season of life is over, He allows us to sit back and wonder in amazement how it all happened. The fruit borne by divine appointments, often times cannot be seen up close, but as the seasons of life roll on, one can only stand in amazement of God's incredible tapestry woven through our lives during this brief visit to planet Earth combined with those whom He has divinely chosen for us to meet!

Today the land of Israel is dotted with youth groups and youth worship bands that came out of Souled Out's ministry. Even in places where only hatred had once ruled, youth Bible studies are now flourishing, made up of believing Arabs and Jews together, all a testimony to God's divine timing.

Chapter 5

Ten Days in Hell

"It costs nothing to become a Christian, but it costs everything to be a Christian."

God's direction for my life had become much clearer. My focus, passion, and calling had seemed to shift overnight. What He was about to do with me, I didn't know for sure, but I was glad to be along for the ride! One thing that had become clearer was that my calling involved other nations and ministry opportunities that I had never dreamed of. I was an ordinary person that God was about to bless with extraordinary experiences!

While ministry in Israel was beginning to occupy my time and passion, it didn't seem logical to even consider another possibility of travel and ministry somewhere else. But God's ways are not ours, and in February 1995, Phil, the same gentleman that had taken our family to Israel, asked me if I would like to go with him and a World War II holocaust survivor to the 50th anniversary celebration of the American liberation of Buchenwald concentration camp in Eastern Germany by American soldiers. There, 80,000 Jews, Christians, and political prisoners had perished in Hitler's gas chambers and ovens. And now, some 5,000 survivors were gathering,

along with 38 American soldiers who were part of that liberation. Joe, the camp survivor, and I would raise the number of
Americans to 41.

Little did I realize that by being part of the celebration, I
would find myself walking back into the pages of history,
reliving the horrors of those brave men and women, who
experienced personally, Hitler's "Final Solution," for the Jews.

It was a cold and blustery day as our plane landed in
Frankfurt, Germany.

Joe was an interesting individual. Though the war had
ended 50 years before, his experiences still haunted and
affected him greatly. Almost every night, we would be awakened by his screams as he relived memories of those tortuous
days 50 years before. Joe had been in charge of collecting
the corpses of those who had died overnight. Each morning,
after standing at roll call for two hours, his job had been to
go to every barrack and remove the dead bodies of those
who hadn't made it to roll call and take them to the ovens for
cremation.

As we left the airport in a rented car, we were immediately made aware that whatever God had in mind for us at
Buchenwald, would be immediately challenged by the enemy.
We no sooner left the parking deck and emerged into traffic
when a huge piece of metal from a passing truck hit our windshield on the driver's side, and if it hadn't been for the shatter
proof windshield, Phil, could have been seriously injured or
even killed. My first reaction was, "Welcome to Germany!" I
knew the spiritual arena that we were entering contained the
murder of 80,000 Jews and Christians at Buchenwald, but
our near disaster brought home the fact that such demonic
activity was still active.

The first concentration camps in Germany were built
after the mass arrests, which accompanied Hitler's seizure
of power in 1933. The concentration camp on Ettersberg Hill
near Weimar was founded in 1937. The decision to select this
site was made because it was close to Weimar. This clas-
sical German town, known for its contribution to German lit-

erature, had been overrun by German Socialists, otherwise known as Nazis. Now, just 8 kilometers north from Weimar, the name Buchenwald (Beech Forest), would be engraved on the world's mind forever.

We could see it on the faces of the people in Weimar, the village at the foot of the mountain where Buchenwald had been built. The blank stares and lack of emotion and feeling belied the guilt and pain of those who lived there. During the days when the camp was a killing machine, the town's people had been told that the camp was producing electricity. Even with the giant furnaces burning thousands of bodies which produced thick white smoke from their chimneys; even with the valley below silted with fine white dust that looked like snow but in fact was charred bone fragments, most Germans denied knowing anything about the camp's activities. Even when the war was over and Buchenwald liberated, that lack of knowledge was challenged by what American commander General Patton made the townspeople do. Early one morning, he made them march up the hilly road to Buchenwald. Video footage shows the people laughing and seemingly enjoying the hike. But after leaving the camp, where the towns people witnessed the piles of dead bodies, corpses still half cremated in the furnaces, the piles of human hair used for stuffing pillows, the tables filled with extracted gold teeth, and the approximately 21,000 starved prisoners barely alive, a much different picture developed. As the people emerged from the heavy iron gates, which contained the caption "Jedem das Seine" (Each to his own; everyone gets what he deserves), their faces of laughter turned to horror and disbelief. How such an atrocity could have taken place and nobody knew? That question has been left to the ages and is still debated.

I will never forget my experience at the death camp and after being there for one week, I felt as if I had been taken back in time and was experiencing what I had only read about in history books.

Because East Germany was still far behind the West economically, Buchenwald had only recently been somewhat renovated. Yet much of the grounds were still very similar to the war days. I remember several brick and wooden barracks that still stood, and looking in, could only imagine what had taken place there. How many stories of valor as well as suffering could never be calculated. Then there were the torture rooms and instruments used for torture. Their very natures are almost too graphic to write about. I remember the giant smokestack, from which the white smoke had billowed forth spewing white bone ash over the valley below. Some who lived in Weimar then have described it like having a snow storm in July, with the ground actually being covered with white ash. I will never forget the "experimental room," where young Jewish children were used in medical experiments often times being operated on while alive with little or no sedative. Then there was the death block. Anyone who entered there immediately knew that there would never be a release. Walking down those narrow halls, I witnessed cell after cell, some actually still containing personal effects of those who had been prisoners and ultimately killed. It was in one of those cells that a picture on the wall got my attention. It was of a young man, maybe in his 30's. His name was Paul Schneider a member and pastor of the Confessional Church. The church had been co-founded by the Reverend Martin Niemoller who opposed the Nazis. Niemoller is remembered for this famous quote: "First they came for the Communists, but I was not a Communist, so I didn't speak up. Then they came for the trade unionists, but I was not a trade unionist, so I didn't speak up. Then they came for the Jews, but I was not a Jew, so I didn't speak up. Then they came for me, and there was no one left to speak for me." What I remember about Paul's picture was his eyes; they seemed to look right through me. It got even more interesting when I heard his story. Paul Schneider had been jailed at camp Buchenwald on November 27, 1937, shortly after the camp had opened. After being sentenced to solitary confinement, he would still preach to his fellow prisoners from the window of his prison cell. Each time he shared the Gospel, he was beaten. Many prisoners pleaded with him to stop preaching and not provoke the SS, but the beatings and torture could not stop him from sharing the Good News. On July 18, 1939, Paul Schneider was murdered with a lethal injection of strophanthin in the camp infirmary. He had been sent into the death house to die by starvation, but after two weeks of watching him seemingly grow stronger in his worship and faith, his guards became fearful and chose death by poisoning. Even in the last days of his life and death, Paul's spiritual courage had defied the hellish circumstances that surrounded him. The scripture on his cell wall defined his faith, walk, and desire to serve Christ. It read, "So we are Christ's ambassadors, as if God Himself were speaking through us. We beg you for His sake, to lay hold of the Divine favor and be reconciled to God."

Despite Gestapo surveillance, many hundreds of Paul's family and friends attended his funeral, including many members of the Confessing Church. At the graveside the words of the pastor described the legacy that Paul Schneider would leave to so many. "May God grant that the witness of your shepherd, our brother, remain with you and continue to impact future generations, and that it remain vital and bear fruit in the entire church."

I had never met Paul Schneider, but staring into his empty cell and coming to understand the fullness of love and joy that motivated him to remain faithful to Christ, was for me a divine appointment of the highest magnitude, for his legacy mirrored my strongest aspiration and desire to model Christ.

So many more experiences, too numerous to mention took place during my week's stay there. I will never forget the videotaped interviews that I was blessed to take. Russians and Poles, Ukrainians and Hungarians; everyone had a story to tell. People from every walk of life and nationality filled the grounds of Buchenwald and the giant welcome tent where the prisoners were fed like kings and queens, every kind of food imaginable. It was the government's way of saying just how sorry they were for the lives and time, which had been stolen and the pain inflicted upon these men and women who now were reaching the end of life's journey. How ironic that the tent was located right next to the original housing for the SS guards and Nazis commanders.

You might now think that my experience could not contain any more drama, but we were only getting started. It was late one evening, and both Phil and I decided to venture into town and find a restaurant. We ended up in a small and quaint German café. It was rather quiet and dark, and except for a middle-aged gentleman to our left, was pretty empty. After we had ordered dinner, we decided to introduce ourselves to the man sitting by himself. Much to our surprise, he immediately identified himself as an American from Indiana. John was a farmer and as we were to find out had an amazing story to tell.

He too had come to Buchenwald for the anniversary of the camp's liberation. But his reason for being there was quite different than ours. Instead of being a former prisoner, he actually was one of 38 Americans who had in fact helped to liberate Buchenwald, whom the German government had invited back for the 50 year anniversary. Not only was John a part of the liberation, but he was one of the first American soldiers through the front gate that fateful April day in 1945.

As John seemed to measure his words, I could tell they were not coming easy and the depth of pain from that experience still overwhelmed him. Our questions weren't making it any easier. "What was it like? What did you first see? How did it affect you?" John answered as best he could but finally just broke down in tears. "Look," he said, "I've not told anyone about this part of my life...ever! Neither my parents nor my wife know just what I saw." Then, as if on cue, he began to pour out his heart. The Holy Spirit had divinely arranged this night for John's deliverance from the past and healing for his heart and future.

In the midst of many tears and times of dead silence, John began to relate his story. "As we climbed the hill towards Buchenwald that cool and calm morning, the sound of American and German gun fire seemed to engulf the beautiful German country side. Our commanders had told us that the fortress at the top, with the huge brick smokestacks was a power plant, and we had no reason to doubt." He continued, "As I reached the summit, there was the large edifice looming in front of me with a huge iron gate. Above the gate, was a giant clock that was permanently stopped at the exact time of the camp's liberation at 3:15 PM. I rushed through the gate only to witness German SS and other soldiers, scurrying out the back. Once inside, we began to move towards a large building that seemed to house something sinister. I could smell the stench of burning flesh, which I had experienced many times before." It was at that point that this young Indiana farm kid became a man. He continued, "I turned a corner into a courtyard and saw three large pits approximately 40-50 feet across directly in front of me. To my horror, they were filled with human bodies some containing no skin and little flesh. Many were already dead but some were still moving. With my body trembling, I turned away and stumbled through the door of a large adjacent building. And what I witnessed there will forever be seared in my heart and soul. In front of me, were the cremation ovens that the Germans had fled from just minutes earlier. There were the bodies, some half stuffed in the ovens and others severely burned and hanging out the oven's doors. I will never forget the looks of horror and pain on the faces of those who had become the victims of Hitler's brutality. I will also never forget the chimneys with the plumes of white smoke flowing from their tops. My experience at Buchenwald changed just how I view life forever, and I am only telling you now to honor my brave comrades who never made it home like I did."

I was later to find out that there were approximately 6 crematoriums and smoke stacks on camp Buchenwald. And because of their continual use, both day and night, the human body fat would collect so thickly on the inside of the chimney, that guards would climb latters, and scrape off into buckets the built up fat along the inside walls. That fat was then placed on pieces of moldy bread and fed to prisoners.

Early the next morning, I accompanied Joe down to those crematoriums so that he could place some candles and flowers before the huge crowd arrived. Our walk from the intimidating gate entrance, where we had parked, was an interesting experience, to say the least. It was a short ten-minute walk, but for Joe, it seemed like an eternity, because the last time he had traveled down this path, he had been a prisoner with no rights and no life left to live. How ironic now, that the same country, which had murdered so many family members and other people dear to him, was now honoring him as a hero.

As we began the walk, the parade grounds loomed in front of us. With the wind whistling and the chill in the air making our light jackets basically useless, Joe's description of what took place on the grounds felt all to surreal. Exactly at 4:00 am every morning, each prisoner was marched to the parade grounds and stood at strict attention for hours as roll call was read. If a guard saw a prisoner so much as blink, they were pulled out of line and shot on the spot. To make this experience even more unbearable was the tissue thin clothing worn by the prisoners. German winters were bitterly cold and many prisoners died standing up while waiting for their names to be read. Then, we came upon an old wooden wagon that had been used to carry the dead bodies to the crematoriums. It was like the very one that Joe had used to carry out his grisly duties every morning. In fact, it could have been the very one. We soon passed a small brick amphitheater, which wasn't used for drama but a place of macabre entertainment for German SS and Gestapo officers and their families. Each Sunday after attending church, the officers and their wives and children came to the amphitheater on the grounds of Buchenwald and were entertained by watching emaciated Jewish prisoners torn limb from limb by giant Russian brown bears towering at least eight feet tall. On a tree, by the circular amphitheater, was a picture of one of the bears kept at Buchenwald for the soldier's entertainment. For added enjoyment on those Sunday excursions, each child was allowed to pick out one Jew to be hanged right there before the cheering crowd's eyes.

Just before we arrived at the crematoriums, Joe stopped by a giant caged in area covered by undergrowth. He stopped and stared in disbelief as if what he was viewing could never have happened. In a very angry but saddened voice, he looked at me and said, "There's where they kept 'dem damn dogs'." With those words, he pulled back his shirt sleeve to reveal a forearm that had a huge chunk of bone and tissue missing. One day just for amusement, a guard had unleashed a large German shepherd dog, which had chewed off half of Joe's arm. One might wonder just how humanity could sink to such a debased moral state, but you must keep in mind that Hitler had convinced many of his countrymen that Jews were not human beings and therefore had no rights in the Third Reich. And because they were considered a danger to the Nazis government, they deserved everything that they received.

As we entered the building, I immediately noticed a strange smell. Much to my chagrin, it smelled like a summer time barbecue back home. Of course, with the profound historical events that had taken place here, my imagination was subject to all sorts of subjective thoughts and behavior. So I simply disregarded the smell as nothing. A few minutes later John, came through the doors. As tears streamed down his face, I asked him his thoughts. His response was not what I had anticipated. "It's not the ovens that are getting to me but the smell. It smells exactly as it did the evening that I first entered through the doors!" I stood there overwhelmed with emotion. Later back home, it took me 6 months to get that smell out of my mind and off my clothes. In fact, I took my suit to the cleaners several times, in hopes that they could remove the smell, whether imaginary or real. And to this day, backyard barbecues as well as eating meat still bother me.

Our relationship with John did not end there. Within the year, he came to our church in Ohio, along with his wife to visit and share his testimony. Not being a public speaker, John was rather shy, but when he entered the pulpit, the Holy Spirit took over and so blessed our church, that there was hardly a dry eye in the sanctuary.

John had gone to Germany in hopes of dealing with his past; a past that had haunted his dreams and thoughts for years. But instead, he met Jesus Christ, the resurrector of dreams through one divinely inspired meeting, late one night in a German café.

I could include so many more brave testimonies that I was privileged to video; I could relate so many more divine appointments that will bless me for eternity. But one thing will forever be the most impacting experience of my trip; how the Holy Spirit would take Phil and me all the way to Eastern Germany to be a vehicle of healing and restoration for a soldier who needed one more victory—putting to death the ghosts of Buchenwald and receiving his new life and future that Jesus had waiting for him.

Chapter 6

Mission Impossible

"Only those who dare to fail
greatly can ever achieve greatly."
Robert Francis Kennedy

August 2002 was one of the most exciting moments in my life. History Maker 1 was about to convene in Limassol, Cyprus. Youth from Cyprus, Jordan, Syria, Ukraine, Egypt, Kuwait, Lebanon, and Israel...yes Israel were about to come together on that beautiful island paradise for one week of restoration and reconciliation. Each delegate was a believer in Yeshua (or Jesus), but politically they were centuries and miles apart. Our goal was simple: to be History Makers between the nations of the Middle East, planting the Gospel of peace and healing. We had a desire to achieve what no peace treaty could ever accomplish; we were naïve enough to believe that the love of Christ could bring down the very highest dividing wall that separated Jew from Arab. We saw ourselves as fighting the "war on terror" at a grass roots level by first changing the hearts of men.

But getting to Cyprus was just as amazing as the conference itself. It was a late afternoon, and I found myself on a narrow country road just outside of L'viv Ukraine, with

Pastor Taras, who was a close friend and pastor of our "sister" church in L'viv. As we were riding along on our way to a youth meeting, Pastor Taras was sharing several important issues with me, but I just couldn't concentrate. My mind seemed to wander in all sorts of directions (which is not uncommon), but I just figured it was from that strong Ukrainian coffee that I had just been force-fed by my friends. I had a restless night of sleep and had experienced several dreams that had left a lingering impact, but I couldn't remember what they were. Then something very strange happened. It was like watching a scary movie, or reading an exciting book. Pastor Taras began by asking me a question that would affect the course of my life forever. He no sooner said the first words than I realized what he was asking me was what I had dreamed the night before. "Pastor Chuck," he began, "I have been asked to teach at a Christian college in Armenia in June for two weeks, but I cannot go. Would you consider going and speaking for me?" Armenia?? It might as well have been in the middle of the Amazon rainforest, for all I knew. Even though I was a student of history, I barely knew where Armenia was located. If it wasn't for Noah's ark and Mt. Ararat located near there, I would have felt really stupid. Taras had no idea that when I got back home from Ukraine, I only had several weeks to raise $15,000.00 for the Cyprus conference, and fundraising was not one of the gifts of the Holy Spirit that I had been blessed with. So his question was answered in my mind with a resounding no, but in my heart, there was a joy that only the Holy Spirit could produce. I sensed God speaking to me in that soft gentle voice letting me know that, if I would step out in faith, he had an adventure waiting for me and would take care of all finances.

I was home a very short time, and while I should have been thinking of ways to raise money for History Maker, I was packing my bags for Armenia and God's divine appointment that would be waiting for me there. I remember thinking that God had better be in this little detour, or my name would be mud!

The plane trip to Armenia was rather eventful. Due to bad weather and a missed flight in Cincinnati, Ohio, we missed each of our next connecting flights, culminating with my co-traveler and I being locked up in a Russian hotel in Moscow for three days with two armed guards, which I will share about later. When we finally got to Yerevan Armenia, our driver was leaving the airport, after waiting for three days for our arrival. By God's grace, we ran into him as he was walking out.

I had been promised by the school's administrator, that while I was in Armenia, I could use his computer to raise funds back in the states for History Maker. Upon arrival, I was informed that I no longer had that as an option. So here I was, no more than a few weeks from leaving for Cyprus, sitting in a small Armenian apartment and still needing $15,000.00 and with no means of solving the problem. So what I did was put together a very sophisticated and deep felt prayer to God that many of us pray in moments like this...HELP!!!!!!!!

What happened next during my stay in Armenia can only be described as a "God Thing". I can truly say that obedience to a simple dream and the tugging of the Holy Spirit, not only gave me an Armenian family, which I will discuss about in the next chapter, but also raised my faith to a whole new level to go home and trust God for $15,000.00 in just a few short days.

I think back now, some 8 years later, and I cannot say that when I arrived back in the States, after my two week's stay in Armenia, that I had any doubt about raising the money. But when it came down to one day before we needed the money for plane tickets for our Israeli delegation, I began to panic. It is in those moments, when our flesh wants to take over, allowing fear to set in, that Jesus responds, "Peace be still."

It was a typical Sunday morning worship service, except that it was the last Sunday before we were to leave for Cyprus. I had mentioned in service that we needed a miracle and very soon but most people didn't know how big. The money had to be wired to Israel on Monday, and our group was leaving on Wednesday. God might not be too soon, but He is never late, as I was about to learn. One of our students, who was going to

Cyprus, asked if he could give a testimony about our reasons for doing History Maker. His words were anointed and well received, but were they too little and too late?

After church, I was going to my car, and a newly married young couple approached me and stated that they wanted to help with the conference. My first reaction was one of thankfulness, but what difference could such a young couple make? They asked to come in Monday morning and see me. In the meantime, Monday arrived, and I called our Israeli leaders in Tel Aviv and gave them the news that we did not have the money to wire them. Their response was a resounding, "Let's pray." I did mention that a young couple wanted to donate, but their two or three hundred dollars would only scratch the surface. What good would an Israeli Arab conference be without the Israelis, I began to ask myself.

Soon, there was a knock at my door and in came the young couple. After ten minutes of small talking, the young man looked at me and asked, "How much do you need?" How much? I remember thinking that, son, you have no clue. He prodded me again, and I gave him the amount. Without even wincing, he turned to his wife and said, "Write the check." My neck shot back so quickly that I nearly had whiplash. I had an emotional breakdown on the spot, as did they, but the greatest shout of joy was when I called Tel Aviv and broke up their prayer meeting with the good news. To this day, I still believe their shouting could be heard clear across the Atlantic! But God still had one more miracle in store.

I went home utterly exhausted from the morning's activities and was just about to relax, when the same young man who had given the Sunday morning testimony, called and gave me some discouraging news. Oh I of little faith felt the pangs of panic begin to settle in again when he said that, as our Cyprus trip accountant, there was some clerical error with the airlines, and we were still $4,000.00 short. Well, it might as well have been $40,000.00 because many Israeli students from the north of the country were already making their way south to the airport in Tel Aviv, and we had to have the money wired the next day.

When I get in situations that are beyond my control, and where I just don't have an answer, I go into my garden and pull weeds. I despise weeds. Some people go into their prayer closet, I pull weeds. While I was pulling every thistle in sight, my secretary called and said that some lady wanted to talk to me. I thought that it was a friend in Texas, but she said, "No, it was the lady you just met with." My life passed in front of my eyes. Why would she be calling me back? One thing was for sure; I would never tell her that we still needed more money. I was allowing my pride to get in the way of the Holy Spirit. "How is the trip planning going," she began. I told her that we were forging ahead. Without mincing any more words she then said, "Ok, how much more do you need?" I was speechless, which doesn't happen very often. I glibly said, "$4,000.00" She said, "I'll meet you at the office in 20 minutes." The Holy Spirit had made known to her our need and in a moment's time, He was faithful to meet our need.

God had used a dream to get me to Armenia to increase my faith, and now he was building it even more through a young couple, who listened to God and would be key instruments in helping to heal prejudice and hatred among 80 young people, who made up History Maker I. But Cyprus was only half of the story, because the events leading up to Cyprus, in Armenia, form another part of a story that was simply amazing.

Chapter 7

Who Would Have Believed It?

"One act of obedience is better than 100 sermons."
Dietrich Bonheoffer

History Maker I was looming on the horizon, and a good sum of money had to still be raised. So what was I doing flying to Vanadzor, Armenia to speak at a college for two weeks, when I needed to be home raising money? I've often asked myself that question. But because it didn't make sense, it made perfect sense, in the scheme of things as to how the Holy Spirit seemed to move in my life. I had come to expect the unexpected and then watch God move in the impossible. As stated in the previous chapter, when Pastor Taras, of Bethesda Church in L'viv Ukraine, had asked me to replace him on a two week teaching odyssey in Armenia, I responded in the affirmative due to a dream that I had had the night before; a dream where I had been asked to travel and teach somewhere. In my dream, I didn't know the location or who was asking, but I knew that I had to go in obedience. What would transpire was truly an act of the Holy Spirit that brought two unlikely churches into a relationship that has touched many lives on two different continents.

It was raining and storming when we landed in Cincinnati, Ohio, and soon all flights were being cancelled or delayed. That began a chain reaction for us that caused us to miss all of our connecting flights in Europe. The end result was being placed in a Moscow hotel with guards for three days, until the next available flight to Vanadzor. Words cannot express what it was like experiencing a modern day version of the Gulag, having our every move monitored.

Monday could not come soon enough. As we were escorted to the airport by our chaperones, who thought that they were the reincarnation of the infamous KGB, we could only thank God for getting us out of Moscow. Because we were arriving three days late in Yerevan the capitol of Armenia, we had no idea what had happened to the school official who was to pick us up and drive us the two and one half hours to Vanadzor. Again, where God leads, He provides. Just as we had come through baggage claim and were considering our next move, a young man who was leaving the airport, turned to my friend and asked if we were Americans. Well, he was the young man sent to pick us up and had just decided to give up and go back to Vanadzor when he recognized us by our dress. Those American flag t-shirts will do it every time!

I have come to learn that the Holy Spirit will reveal one thing to you for the express purpose of revealing something greater. I thought that I was going to teach in a school, but the Holy Spirit had something far bigger in mind.

It was a rough ride up the mountains to get to Vanadzor, yet it was one of the most majestic and beautiful experiences that I had ever had. From Mt. Ararat rising in the distance, to the pristine mountains covered with wild flowers, to the deep emerald blue valleys glistening with the early morning dew, Armenia was a vista of beauty to behold.

We arrived at our place of lodging and early the next morning the classes began. I always prided myself on being able to communicate with college students, but even though my students spoke English, I could not break through. At first

I thought that maybe it was cultural, but soon discerned that it was a bigger issue.

The students had been having problems with the school administration, and because I was brought in by the school head, the natural assumption was that I was one of them. Finally, on the fourth day of class, a young man by the name of Varo, stood and spoke for the class. He had been a sniper in the Russian army and had killed many men, but now he had come to know Jesus. So when Varo wanted to speak, I readily gave him the floor. "Pastor," he began, "We want to know your connections to the school leadership and if you are like them." Boy was that a loaded question! Well, because the school was run by a foreign church organization, I wasn't going to get in the middle of an international squabble. I carefully chose my words and told them that I had just met the school superintendent and was not part of their denomination. Well, that was all it took. The students mobbed me with hugs and tears and wrote on the board USA...USA...!

All the walls soon came down, and I was being invited to speak in many local churches. Several days later, a young girl named Nara approached me and said that her father-in-law, who was a pastor, would like to meet me. It was like many other invitations; however this one seemed different. Once we met, we immediately became like long lost family and formed a relationship that even still today is thriving and growing.

When I first went to their church to speak, it was during their worship that I began to connect the dots all the way back to my dream in the Ukraine that had led me to Armenia. Because of my financial obligations for History Maker I, as stated, I had no good reason to be going to Armenia, except that God said, "Go and I will bless you!" I was staring at part of that blessing. The worship was very powerful and joy-filled and seemed to take away all my anxieties about fund raising when I got home. Even the words spoken during the service, seemed to build my faith letting me know that, as my faith was being tested, the Holy Spirit was preparing me for an incredibly far-reaching experience in Cyprus during History

Maker. Then after service, I told the pastor's son, Arman, that I sensed he would be traveling a lot and coming to America. He looked at me in disbelief and stated that only a week or two before, someone had told him the exact same thing. To this point in time, he had never traveled.

As my stay in Armenia came to an end, God had one more special blessing in store for me. As we were on our way back to the airport and nearing Mt. Ararat, I thought to myself how wonderful it would be to travel so close to Ararat and see a rainbow. We had been by the place where Mt. Ararat could be viewed many times during my stay, but it was always cloudy and rainy. So I didn't have much faith that my ride to the airport would be any different. I will always remember that trip, because, as we approached Ararat, I had fallen asleep to the pitter-patter of rain on our vehicle. But something strange happened. We had come around a sharp curve, and I had sat up only to feel the warmth of sunlight on the back of my neck. It began as a silver lining, far into the distance behind me. But the faint line began to grow, and before I knew it, we were engulfed with billowing white clouds and blue sky overhead. Then it happened as if on cue. To my left, deep into the valley below me, brilliant colors of radiant light began to arch over and around us. Then a second pattern began to form. Suddenly, as our driver pulled to the side of the road, we sat there speechless as a canopy of colors, like waving bands of ribbons, formed not one but two giant rainbows. They stretched from mountain to mountain and valley to valley so vast that words could never describe their beauty. Nara, the pastor's daughter-in law, was riding in the front, and I said to her, after I gained my composure, that I could not imagine living in such a place of beauty and experiencing such rainbows on a regular basis. "Pastor," she began, "We have never seen such rainbows like this. In all of my living days, I have never seen this." The colors were layered so that at least five brilliant shades were visible, with the deepest being purple. I was later to learn that whenever a rainbow included the deepest shades of purple, it was considered the most unique and impressionistic. Well, after we were on our way, Nara, turned to me and said, "Pastor, we have not met by accident. God has something great in store and the rainbow, like with Noah, has sealed our relationship forever!"

When the Holy Spirit says, "Trust me...just trust me," it is because He has something much greater in store that cannot be seen at the moment. In the greater design of what He is weaving, oftentimes it might not be initially recognized, yet something truly divine is happening, and along the way, you might just have a few divine appointments; maybe even a rainbow!

And by the way, guess where History Maker II convened in June 2010? It was held in the least likely of all places-Vanadzor, Armenia where 140 youth from 8 different nations attended for 4 days; all because of a dream, an offer, a rainbow and a few divine appointments along the way!

It has been 8 years since that first trip to Armenia, and to say the least, God has been faithful to His Word. Pastor Arman has ministered many times in our church as well as in Europe and India. Likewise, we have had numerous teams visit Armenia for all sorts of mission activities culminating with History Maker II in June 2010.

Because of a dream in Ukraine, a relationship was formed in Armenia giving wings to History Maker I in Cyprus and History Maker II in Armenia—all because of God's divine appointments and numerous believers seeking to hear His voice along the way!

Epilogue

Keys to Experiencing Divine Appointments

"When a man is willing and eager, God joins in."
Aeschylus

I have often been asked about the unique ways in which I have met people and the amazing stories that have followed. I can most assuredly tell you that it has had nothing to do with any special intelligence or gifting that I possess. If that were the case, most divine appointments in my life would never have happened. However, what is true are the words of Saint Paul in 2nd Timothy chapter 4, when he challenges his spiritual son, Timothy, to always be ready to do the work of an evangelist whether gifted as one or not.

Evangelism can take place in many ways, but let me share with you what I have gleaned from the teachings of Jesus concerning making a difference in someone's life. He had a way of meeting strangers, seeing into their hearts and changing their lives. Because He was God, He knew everything to begin with, yet He humbled Himself as a man and ministered to each person individually. Maybe you have asked the question, "How can I become a candidate for God to place divine appointments in my path?" I want to conclude by answering that question.

First of all, we must see evangelism and discipleship as part of the same process—a commitment involving time and sacrifice and not just a one-time spiritual event where we get another notch on our spiritual belt. I would much rather commit my time and energies to bringing about change in one or two lives per year than speaking to thousands. I have been blessed to do both, and I can tell you that nothing is more rewarding than watching a person who did not believe that change was possible, experience the freedom that Christ offers and put that new found hope and courage into action. Think about what Jesus modeled for us. He took a band of nondescript individuals, whom the world deemed as unfit for anything extraordinary, and in the space of three years' time, transformed their lives through spending time with them. It so revolutionized their lives that they, in turn birthed a spiritual revolution that transformed the Roman Empire.

Secondly, we must make ourselves available. I'm not just talking about praying a simple prayer every morning like, "Jesus, please use me today." While that sort of prayer is powerful and can move mountains, it must be matched with a passion that cries out for the brokenhearted along with a passionate desire to share the truth that brings restorative healing and hope. When we are available, every person becomes an opportunity for God's love to be made evident. When we are open, the Spirit gives us a unique sensitivity to discern that soft still voice of God calling us into action. This cannot be learned in a book or taught in a seminar, but can only be found by asking the Holy Spirit to birth a passion for the lost and hurting within our own spirit.

Thirdly, not only must we be available but also alert to the events unfolding around us. Recently, while in a grocery checkout line, a lady standing behind me had just three items. Since my cart was full, I asked her if she wanted to go ahead of me. My desire was to be courteous, but God had placed her behind me for a reason. She was very appreciative and told me that she had a plane to catch and was getting short on time. Suddenly, I knew that a "God thing" was about to happen. I asked her where she was flying to and there, between my green beans and her bag of chips and pop, she related how she had come to visit her mother who was very ill. She had been here for some time but had to fly home to take care of some personal business before coming back. I could see the stress on her face and responded by telling her that I was a pastor and would be praying for her mom. When I gave her my card and told her to have her mother call if she needed me, her eyes filled with tears, and she told me that she had felt so alone and discouraged and was asking God for strength to cope. Our brief time together had restored her peace and joy, and now she was prepared for her journey home. Her mother never called, and I have never seen the lady since. However, because I was alert enough to sense her pain and not so concerned to get out of the grocery line, (which I always detest), the Holy Spirit was able to use me in a very small way. I knew in my heart that I had just experienced a divine appointment that had ministered to a broken and exhausted heart.

Fourth, being a good listener is foundational for developing trust in any new relationship. As a young pastor and also being somewhat overwhelmed by people and their circumstances, I developed a very bad habit that was completely shattered one Sunday morning. I was talking to a lady and at the same time observing four other people standing behind her waiting to talk with me. I heard her words, but they were not reaching my heart, and my face showed it. I passively responded to her question and was ready to talk to the next person in line. The following day she called me and in no uncertain terms let me know that she had felt like a number and very unimportant. I might have answered her question, but I had not gained her trust. With Jesus, it always seemed that each person He ministered to was the most important person in His life. I'm sure they felt important, because He didn't give them spiritual formulas for success, but touched their very core with truth and healing. Consider the woman at the well or the woman caught in adultery. How about little Zaccheus or Peter the Prideful? Then there was Thomas the doubter and Lazarus and an empty tomb. In each case, Jesus ministered to them as if no one else existed. As God positions people in our lives, we must treat them with respect and honor them with our full attention. It is then that true relationship is formed, which forms the basis for taking that person to the next level.

Fifth, I want to talk about that word "relationship," because there is a philosophy that I try to live by when meeting new people. First of all, I have experienced many "divine appointments" which have passed through my life and then are gone just as quickly. The individual and I met for a reason, and once that need was met, oftentimes I rarely saw that person again. Yet occasionally, I will meet someone that I know has been placed in my life for a much longer period of time, if not forever. It is that individual that I want to briefly talk about and share my philosophy on building solid trust-based relationships. Most importantly, I believe that I do not have the right to speak into someone's life until I have gained their trust. I'm not talking about giving advice or direction; we do that with strangers. What I am talking about is digging deep into the person's heart and soul and challenging the darkness, while offering God's restorative hope and healing. This involves the sacrifice of time and patience. I personally cannot intrude into the inner recesses of someone's life or make "religious" judgments until I know that the person is ready to trust me at that level. That is why hard-core evangelism is not always the best approach. Today's generation doesn't respond to Christian clichés, because most are looking for authentic relationships and not old worn-out religious arguments and judgmental attitudes. Most already know that their lives are filled with pain and sin and they don't need us reminding them. What I am talking about is central to not only having a divine encounter, but developing a real and vibrant relationship that can last a lifetime.

Sixth, while relational bridge-building is a key for divine appointments to flourish, what transpires next is just as important-follow up. For any friendship to grow through the seasons of life, time becomes the key ingredient for success. Almost all of my closest friendships have been forged through crazy divine encounters, yet the hardest thing has been to find quality time to spend so that each person might know that he or she is valued and special. I am the first to admit that I have not always been sensitive to my friends' needs. Just remember that it is crucial, especially when a new relationship is in the developmental stages, that you promise only what you can fulfill, yet at the same time trying to be as compassionate, authentic, and real as possible. More than once I have been challenged by a close friend, whom I have lost contact with because of circumstances. Nothing can be worse than someone feeling that they were simply your yearly project, which has now been completed. Remember that we are the only "Jesus" that some people see and touch. Especially during spiritual infancy, new believers need our love and support. Your sacrifice of time and love now will produce a spiritual harvest later that will last a lifetime.

I want to conclude by briefly discussing one of Jesus' most incredible divine appointments and see just how one moment in time changed a whole village. The story is found in John chapter 5 where Jesus spends time with a Samaritan woman at Jacob's well and astonishes her with His deep understanding of her sorted lifestyle. The disciples had gone to town looking for food, but Jesus stayed behind realizing the opportunity before Him. Samaritans were despised by Jews, and I'm sure that the lady was deeply confused. But this man was so different. He treated her with respect and dignity, and before long, she understood that He was no ordinary man. With utter amazement, as the disciples returned, she rushes back to her village, (a short distance away), leaving her water pots. The disciples were confused as to why Jesus was wasting His time talking to her; their concern had been physical food, but Jesus had something much greater in mind.

When Jesus comes into your life, He positions you for greatness. He has given you the authority to set the captives free. Look at what happened next. The woman had gone back to her village and told anyone who would listen what Jesus had done and who He was. Then Jesus said to His disciples, "My food is to do the will of my Father who sent me...I tell you open your eyes and look at the fields, for they are ripe for harvest." Then, before their very eyes, streaming forth from the village, covering the fields, were the multitudes that one simple Samaritan evangelist with no education but filled with the power of God had shared her faith with. With this powerful example, Jesus revealed to His disciples and to us, that His food is to do the will of His Father and as we choose likewise, He positions us for greatness if we are willing to put self aside. After all, before us stretches fields ripe for harvest. The question then becomes which food are we looking for?

CPSIA information can be obtained at www.ICGtesting.com
Printed in the USA
BVOW071330041011

272736BV00002B/6/P